EYE ON
Art

PUBLIC
ART

Meryl Loonin

LUCENT BOOKS
A part of Gale, Cengage Learning

GALE
CENGAGE Learning

Detroit • New York • San Francisco • New Haven, Conn • Waterville, Maine • London

LIBRARY OF CONGRESS CATALOGING-IN-PUBLICATION DATA

Loonin, Meryl.
  Public art / by Meryl Loonin.
    pages cm. -- (Eye on art)
  Summary: "These books provide a historical overview of the development of different types of art and artistic movements; explore the roots and influences of the genre; discuss the pioneers of the art and consider the changes the genre has undergone"-- Provided by publisher.
  Includes bibliographical references and index.
  ISBN 978-1-4205-0917-5 (hardback)
 1. Public art--Juvenile literature. I. Title.
  N8825.L66 2013
  700--dc23
                                          2013039046

Lucent Books
27500 Drake Rd
Farmington Hills MI 48331

ISBN-13: 978-1-4205-0917-5
ISBN-10: 1-4205-0917-9

Printed in the United States of America
1 2 3 4 5 6 7 18 17 16 15 14

CONTENTS

Foreword

"Art has no other purpose than to brush aside . . . everything that veils reality from us in order to bring us face to face with reality itself."
—French philosopher Henri-Louis Bergson

Some thirty-one thousand years ago, early humans painted strikingly sophisticated images of horses, bison, rhinoceroses, bears, and other animals on the walls of a cave in southern France. The meaning of these elaborate pictures is unknown, although some experts speculate that they held ceremonial significance. Regardless of their intended purpose, the Chauvet-Pont-d'Arc cave paintings represent some of the first known expressions of the artistic impulse.

From the Paleolithic era to the present day, human beings have continued to create works of visual art. Artists have developed painting, drawing, sculpture, engraving, and many other techniques to produce visual representations of landscapes, the human form, religious and historical events, and countless other subjects. The artistic impulse also finds expression in glass, jewelry, and new forms inspired by new technology. Indeed, judging by humanity's prolific artistic output throughout history, one must conclude that the compulsion to produce art is an inherent aspect of being human, and the results are among humanity's greatest cultural achievements: masterpieces such as the architectural marvels of ancient Greece, Michelangelo's perfectly rendered statue of *David*, Vincent van Gogh's visionary painting *Starry Night*, and endless other treasures.

The creative impulse serves many purposes for society. At its most basic level, art is a form of entertainment or the means for a satisfying or pleasant aesthetic experience. But art's true power lies not in its potential to entertain and delight but in its ability to enlighten, to reveal the truth, and by doing so to uplift the human spirit and transform the human race.

One of the primary functions of art has been to serve religion. For most of Western history, for example, artists were paid by the church to produce works with religious themes and subjects. Art was thus a tool to help human beings transcend mundane, secular reality and achieve spiritual enlightenment. One of the best-known, and largest-scale, examples of Christian religious art is the Sistine Chapel in the Vatican in Rome. In 1508 Pope Julius II commissioned Italian Renaissance artist Michelangelo to paint the chapel's vaulted ceiling, an area of 640 square yards (535 sq. m). Michelangelo spent four years on scaffolding, his neck craned, creating a panoramic fresco of some three hundred human figures. His paintings depict Old Testament prophets and heroes, sibyls of Greek mythology, and nine scenes from the Book of Genesis, including the Creation of Adam, the Fall of Adam and Eve from the Garden of Eden, and the Flood. The ceiling of the Sistine Chapel is considered one of the greatest works of Western art and has inspired the awe of countless Christian pilgrims and other religious seekers. As eighteenth-century German poet and author Johann Wolfgang von Goethe wrote, "Until you have seen this Sistine Chapel, you can have no adequate conception of what man is capable of."

In addition to inspiring religious fervor, art can serve as a force for social change. Artists are among the visionaries of any culture. As such, they often perceive injustice and wrongdoing and confront others by reflecting what they see in their work. One classic example of art as social commentary was created in May 1937, during the brutal Spanish civil war. On May 1 Spanish artist Pablo Picasso learned of the recent attack on the small Basque village of Guernica by German airplanes allied with fascist forces led by Francisco Franco. The German pilots had used the village for target practice, a three-hour bombing that killed sixteen hundred civilians. Picasso, living in Paris, channeled his outrage over the massacre into his painting *Guernica*, a black, white, and gray mural that depicts dismembered animals and fractured human figures whose faces are contorted in agonized expressions. Initially, critics and the public condemned the painting as an incoherent hodgepodge, but the work soon came to be seen as a powerful antiwar statement and remains an iconic symbol of the violence and terror that dominated world events during the remainder of the twentieth century.

The impulse to create art—whether painting animals with crude pigments on a cave wall, sculpting a human form from marble, or commemorating human tragedy in a mural—thus serves many purposes. It offers an entertaining diversion, nourishes the imagination and the spirit, decorates and beautifies the world, and chronicles the age. But underlying all these functions is the desire to reveal that which is obscure—to illuminate, clarify, and perhaps ennoble. As Picasso himself stated, "The purpose of art is washing the dust of daily life off our souls."

The Eye on Art series is intended to assist readers in understanding the various roles of art in society. Each volume offers an in-depth exploration of a major artistic movement, medium, figure, or profession. All books in this series are beautifully illustrated with full-color photographs and diagrams. Riveting narrative, clear technical explanation, informative sidebars, fully documented quotes, a bibliography, and a thorough index all provide excellent starting points for research and discussion. With these features, the Eye on Art series is a useful introduction to the world of art—a world that can offer both insight and inspiration.

Introduction

Art for Everyone

The gigantic steel sculpture by renowned Spanish artist Pablo Picasso rises 50 feet (15.2m) over Daley Plaza in the heart of downtown Chicago, Illinois. When it was first unveiled to the public on August 15, 1967, large crowds gathered to stare up at its towering form. Some told reporters at the scene they thought it was strange or ugly. Others seemed confused by it. They wondered whether the massive artwork, which the artist never named, represented a bird, a modernist portrait of a woman, his beloved dog, or perhaps a baboon. Yet within a decade, the untitled Picasso sculpture had become a popular and highly recognized symbol of the city. It is often seen wearing an enormous Cubs, White Sox, or Bears hat in support of the local sports teams.

What Is Public Art?

The Picasso sculpture is an example of public art—visual art, sculpture, murals, and art installations (that immerse viewers in a three dimensional experience) located outside of museum walls, where everyone can experience the art. Works of public art are found in everyday environments. They can be seen in city plazas and parks, in front of government buildings, libraries, and fire stations, on the National Mall in Washington, D.C., and on subway walls, pedestrian walkways, and bridges. Sometimes they are located in open or public lands in more remote locations where they become destinations for those willing to make the journey: off of country roads, on mountain cliffs, in deserts, stone quarries, or abandoned strip mines. Unlike art displayed in a museum, there is typically no admission fee required to see these works. Public art takes many different forms, from an abstract work made of industrial-strength steel such as Picasso's Chicago sculpture to a black granite memorial wall sunk deep into the earth with the names of soldiers killed in war, from a park with thousands of gates draped with swaths of orange fabric to a grid of tilted mirrors placed on a beach that reveals shimmering snapshots of the ocean's surface. These works have a variety of funding sources, too, including government agencies and taxpayers, private donors, individual artists, or community and nonprofit arts groups. They are permanent or temporary, and, occasionally, placed on abandoned buildings and broken-down walls, old warehouses, and billboards, without permission, in an attempt to reclaim urban spaces for public use.

A New Era in Public Art

Despite the diversity of its forms, materials, and funding sources, for centuries public art served one main purpose: to reinforce the power of ruling elites. Statues, monuments, and triumphal arches in cities around the world preserved and glorified the reigns of monarchs and dictators and celebrated their nations' conquests and victories in war. Members of the ruling classes commissioned decorative art on buildings and fountains as a mark of prestige, to beautify public spaces in the cities where they wielded influence or control.

The Chicago Picasso sculpture represents a new era in public art in the United States that began in the 1960s. As in earlier decades, the newer works were built to beautify cities, many of which had become dismally stark and modern in this

Pablo Picasso's untitled sculpture for Daley Plaza in Chicago, Illinois, is one of the first sculptures commissioned for the city that did not depict a historical figure.

era. But these works were also an attempt to bring art out of the privileged, elite realm of museums, galleries, and private collections and into people's daily lives. At first, this meant exposing the public to the best art outside of museum walls, including abstract sculptures by icons of the modern art world like Pablo Picasso. Except for the fact that they were massive in scale and exhibited out of doors in city parks and plazas, viewing them was a lot like the experience of visiting a modern art museum. Eventually, after several modern, abstract works of sculpture captured national headlines because people found them off-putting or offensive, the emphasis shifted to public art that more successfully engaged its audiences. The *public* in public art became as important as the *art*.

Public Art with an Accent on the Public

In recent decades, works of public art have become interactive, lively, and engaging. They enhance the cities and towns where they are located. They build civic pride, breathe life into poor and neglected neighborhoods, heighten awareness of the environment, and, sometimes, challenge people with bold social or political messages.

More than forty years after the dedication of the untitled Picasso sculpture, Chicago residents often gather around another work of public art, *Crown Fountain*, by Spanish artist Jaume Plensa. It is one of several sculptures in the city's popular Millennium Park, constructed on the site of an abandoned railroad yard and opened to the public in 2004. *Crown Fountain* consists of two 50-foot-tall (15.2m) glass-block towers that stand in a shallow wading pool. The towers are actually giant screens that project a video loop of faces of more than a thousand Chicago residents who represent a cross-section of the city. Sheets of water cascade down every time the screen changes to reveal a new face. Spigots on the towers are lined up with the mouths of the faces, so the mouths appear to be spitting water into the pool below. The sculpture invites interaction and civic engagement. On warm days, it is crowded with visitors of all ages, who sit by the side of the pool conversing, snacking, taking photos, laughing, or cooling off in the spray.

The sheer presence of art outdoors, in public plazas and parks or in front of libraries and office buildings, does not automatically make it public art, explains art historian Cher Krause Knight. Today, there is a new standard. "Art's 'publicness,'" she says, "rests in the quality and impact of its exchanges with audiences."[1]

Evolving Ideas of Public Art

From a granite statue of a Civil War general on horseback to a towering glass fountain that projects video images of human faces, public works of art are found outside of museum walls where everyone can experience them. Throughout American history, these works have inspired patriotism, celebrated victory in war, introduced the public to bold and experimental art forms, breathed new life into rundown cities and neighborhoods, and brought people together to mourn tragic events. The idea of public art is continually evolving to reflect changes in the art world and society at large.

Public artworks today often draw inspiration from the monuments and sculptures of the past, but also incorporate cutting-edge and interactive new technologies. Their forms, materials, and the messages they convey are remarkably diverse. They include an enormous, attention-grabbing stainless steel puppy covered with red and purple flowering plants on display in a busy urban plaza in New York City, a carousel in Tennessee with hand-carved wooden figures of historical characters like Davy Crockett, and a grid of 10-foot-tall (3.05m) nylon rods in Salt Lake City, Utah, that sways with the wind and the movement of people stepping through the rods. These works entertain, send a message, provoke debate, and bring communities together around a shared artistic experience. They are public art not only because they are located in places where people encounter them in their daily lives, says art historian Cher Krause Knight, but also because they "engage their hearts, incite their minds, and risk some discontent along the way."[2]

Statues, Obelisks, and Arches

For much of its early history, America's artists and architects looked to Europe for models of public art. They embellished buildings and parks with decorative ornaments and figures from history and mythology such as cherubs, angels, and gods. They also designed bronze and marble statues to honor former statesmen and military heroes. These works imitated the classical style of monuments in London, Paris, and Rome.

Yet there were also many Americans in the early decades after the nation's founding who frowned on the idea of public art. They identified stone statues with the churches and monarchies of an old, elitist Europe or with false idols, which were strictly forbidden by Puritan religious teachings. The United States government first commissioned a work of public art in 1832 in honor of the centennial of George Washington's birth. The 12-ton (10.89t) marble statue by artist Horatio Greenough was modeled on a likeness of the Greek god Zeus. Greenough portrayed Washington seated on a classical throne, wearing a Greek toga that exposed his bare chest. The work was heavily criticized and ridiculed for its partial nudity and imperial pose. (Greenough's statue originally stood inside the Capitol Rotunda, but

Horatio Greenough's statue of George Washington, the first public art piece commissioned by the U.S. government, is now in the National Museum of American History in Washington, D.C.

was later moved outside because its heavy weight was cracking the floor. It was eventually moved to the Smithsonian Institution, where it remains today.)

Another more ambitious public monument to George Washington was completed in 1885 after four decades of heated debate in the U.S. Congress over its runaway cost and design. No one could agree on the appropriate way to memorialize the iconic first president. The Washington Monument, familiar to most Americans, towers over the capital city in the style of an ancient Egyptian *obelisk* (a stone pillar with a rectangular base and pyramid-shaped top). Many people criticized this monument to the first president just as they had the classical statue by Greenough. "Ah, not this granite, dead and cold,"[3] wrote the nineteenth-century poet Walt Whitman.

Even the Statue of Liberty, dedicated in 1886, did not escape controversy. Some Americans were uncomfortable with the fact that its sculptor, Frederic Bartholdi, was a Frenchman. Although the statue was a gift from France, the U.S. government was responsible for raising the funds for the pedestal at its base. This was highly unpopular at a time when the country was still recovering from a long and costly civil war. The money was eventually raised through benefit events, art auctions, prize-fights, a lottery, and, finally, a direct newspaper appeal. Yet "Lady Liberty," as she came to be known, was dedicated amidst great fanfare and went on to become an emblem of freedom for millions of immigrants who arrived on U.S. shores.

Americans not only rallied around the Statue of Liberty, but also came to accept the idea that the United States should have its own public monuments to inspire patriotism. By the turn of the twentieth century, Washington, D.C. rivaled many European cities in the number and scale of its triumphal monuments, while in smaller cities and towns throughout the country, stone statues appeared in public squares and gardens to honor the lives of local (almost exclusively male) politicians, soldiers, and civil servants. With time, these statues began to fade into the landscape as the heroes and battles they honored were forgotten. Today, most people walk by them with rarely a second glance.

A New Deal for Public Art

Public art took on new meaning and form in the 1930s at the height of the Great Depression, the most devastating economic collapse in U.S. history. It was a time of profound misery and suffering. Millions of Americans lost their jobs and struggled to pay for food, clothing, and housing. Unemployment lines stretched around entire city blocks. Rather than honoring great statesmen or military heroes, the public art of the Depression era was meant to lift the spirits of ordinary Americans and celebrate their contributions to society.

At the height of the economic crisis, President Franklin D. Roosevelt proposed an unprecedented series of government relief and recovery measures intended to create jobs and restore people's pride and faith in the nation. These measures were collectively referred to as the New Deal. Under the New Deal, a federal agency called the Works Progress Administration (WPA) was founded to oversee ambitious programs to distribute food, clothing, and housing, promote literacy, and put Americans back to work.

The New Deal also included the most far-reaching public arts programs ever undertaken by the federal government. From 1933 to 1943, thousands of artists working under the official sponsorship of the U.S. government produced tens of thousands of paintings, sculptures, photographs, plays, and other creative works. Photographers, visual artists, and writers, many of them unemployed and living in poverty, were commissioned to travel across the country and document the diversity of the land and its people. Visual artists were put to work creating murals and sculpture for display in libraries, post offices, schools, parks, and even prisons.

It was not only the massive scale of these arts programs that was unprecedented, but also the ideal behind them: that all citizens, regardless of whether they were laborers, teachers, miners, farmers, or sales clerks, were as entitled to have art and culture in their lives as the wealthiest private art collectors and patrons. Edward Bruce, who headed the Section of Fine Arts at the U.S. Treasury Department during these years, explained:

Our objective should be to enrich the lives of all our people by making things of the spirit, the creation of beauty part of their daily lives, by giving them new hopes and sources of interest to fill their leisure, by eradicating the ugliness of their surroundings, by building with a sense of beauty as well as mere utility, and by fostering all the simple pleasures of life which are not important in terms of dollars spent but are immensely important in terms of a higher standard of living.[4]

Bruce and other New Deal officials devised innovative ways to bring art and culture into people's daily lives. They established percent-for-art guidelines that required that one percent of the total cost of every new federal building under construction should be set aside for artistic decoration of the building's interior and exterior spaces. They also sponsored national competitions for the design of new public artworks, in which the contestants remained anonymous so juries could select the winners on the merits of the designs they submitted and not their status and fame in the art world.

These Depression-era arts programs were innovative and new, but, ironically, the style of art they produced often reflected conventional tastes. New Deal officials promoted works that were realistic and figurative (derived from real life) and discouraged anything that might be perceived as too modern or abstract. Of the more than fourteen hundred murals commissioned for newly built regional post offices, for example, most were painted in an idealized, figurative style that came to be known as *American Scene Painting*. Artists depicted regional scenes, showed New Deal programs at work, and affirmed traditional virtues like hard work and family. The paintings included idyllic scenes of riverboats floating on the Mississippi River, farmers collecting maple sap in a wintry New England landscape, a corn parade in Iowa, and a livestock auction in Colorado. They featured industrial workers, dockhands, blacksmiths, and farmers toiling at their jobs. Although artists tried to please local communities with these scenes, the murals some-

times sparked controversy. Small town residents were offended when out-of-state artists made mistakes in their portrayals of local life or landscapes or showed residents in an unflattering way. The murals also papered over racial and ethnic tensions that laid just below the surface. For example, American Indians were often shown in violent clashes with white settlers, while the role of African Americans in the country's history was played down and the discrimination they faced barely acknowledged. Despite these shortcomings, the program was widely seen as a popular success.

Yet the government's sponsorship of New Deal programs like the post office murals was a temporary measure designed to help people endure the Depression. By the early 1940s, public attention had turned to Europe, which stood on the brink of a

California Life, one of the murals in Coit Tower in San Francisco, California, was among the first works funded by the Public Works of Art Project.

MOUNT RUSHMORE: A MONUMENTAL WORK OF PUBLIC ART

The New Deal era set another precedent in public art with the construction of Mount Rushmore, a monumental work built into the craggy mountains of South Dakota. Mount Rushmore was the dream of a South Dakotan historian named Doane Robinson, who wanted to create a work so impressive that it would become a destination for tourists from across the country. He enlisted a Danish immigrant sculptor, Gutzon Borglum, whose earlier work included a controversial bust of Confederate general Robert E. Lee, carved into a mountain in Georgia with partial funding from the Ku Klux Klan [an anti–African American hate group]. Borglum decided to carve the busts of four great presidents who had helped to preserve and expand the republic: George Washington, Thomas Jefferson, Abraham Lincoln, and Theodore Roosevelt. The chosen site was the tallest mountain in the Black Hills and sacred ground to American Indian tribes, who argued that the land had been seized from them illegally. (In 1946, a local Indian chieftain hired a sculptor to build a competing memorial to the Lakota warrior Crazy Horse, only 17 miles [27.4 km] from Mount Rushmore. Decades later, this massive work remains unfinished.)

For Mount Rushmore, Borglum created the models and invented methods for carving his images into the mountain. More than four hundred unemployed miners were hired to do the heavy work, using jackhammers and dynamite to blast away the rock. Construction started in 1927 and continued for fourteen years. President Franklin Roosevelt first viewed Mount Rushmore in 1936 and found it awe-inspiring. "I had seen the photographs, I had seen the drawings, and I had talked with those who are responsible for this great work," he remarked, "and yet I had no conception, until about ten minutes ago, not only of its magnitude, but also its permanent beauty and importance."

Quoted in Amy Dempsey. *Destination Art*. Berkeley, CA: University of California Press, 2006, p. 35.

devastating war. The ruthless Nazi dictator Adolf Hitler had risen to power in Germany and begun a conquest of neighboring countries in Europe. In 1941, the United States was drawn into the conflict after the Japanese, who sided with the Nazis in the war, bombed Pearl Harbor, Hawaii. The U.S. government began to withdraw its sponsorship of the arts and funnel the money to the mounting war effort. Meanwhile, brutal totalitarian dictators like Hitler in Germany and Joseph Stalin in the Soviet Union, who also rose to power in this era, commissioned monumental works of art and architecture to glorify their regimes. Americans started to regard government sponsorship of the arts with suspicion. For the next twenty years, public art fell into a period of decline.

In the end, the New Deal arts programs were in place for just over a decade, but their impact was long lasting. "They affirmed art's importance in a democratic society," says art historian

The Mount Rushmore National Memorial is carved into the granite face of a mountain in South Dakota.

Knight, "built a significant national collection of public artworks, nurtured creative energies, and laid the groundwork for federal arts funding."[5]

The Best Art Outside Museum Walls

In the 1960s, public art was reinvented again when the federal government renewed its commitment to the arts for the first time since the New Deal. The federal arts programs of the 1960s did not have the massive sweep of those of the 1930s, but they did share the same guiding principles, including the ideas that support for the arts was a legitimate role for a democratic government to play and that all citizens, regardless of their educational backgrounds and incomes, were entitled to have art and culture in their lives. In 1965, under President Lyndon B. Johnson, a new arts agency called the National Endowment for the Arts (NEA) was founded to foster the arts and inspire a sense of national identity and pride. It was a time of tremendous social and political upheaval. The American public was bitterly divided over issues of civil rights, women's liberation, and an escalating war in Vietnam, in which thousands of U.S. troops were fighting and dying. Dramatic changes in music, fashion, and lifestyle also widened the cultural gap between generations. The art world was in turmoil, too, as many artists rejected the elitist world of museums and galleries and began to experiment with new materials and styles. In the world of sculpture, this often meant works that were abstract, geometric, or Minimalist, pared down to the sparest, most essential elements. For the first time, the government commissioned public works of art that were abstract, bold, and often controversial. The goal, according to an influential public arts program run by the NEA called Art in Public Places (AiPP), was "to give the public access to the best art of our time outside museum walls."[6]

The problem was how to interpret the word "best." At first, directors of the federal arts programs turned to the most famous

La Grande Vitesse by Alexander Calder in the City Hall plaza of Grand Rapids, Michigan, is now a symbol of pride for the city.

modern American artists to create sculptures and murals for public spaces. They assumed that these masterworks would fit the spaces anywhere they were placed. It never occurred to the arts program directors to consult with members of the community or consider whether the art had any relevance to them.

One of the first government-sponsored public works of art in this era was a giant bright red abstract sculpture made of industrial steel called *La Grande Vitesse*. It was created by American sculptor and mobile artist Alexander Calder and installed in the city of Grand Rapids, Michigan, in 1969 as part of an effort to beautify a barren-looking plaza near the city hall. (*La Grande Vitesse* translates roughly in French to "Grand Rapids.") The work was sculpted out of flat sheets of Cor-Ten— weatherproof steel—that Calder riveted and welded together in a process similar to that used in ship construction. *La Grande Vitesse* weighed a hefty 42 tons (38.2t) and stood 43 feet high (13.1m). It had to be lifted in pieces and installed in the plaza with heavy cranes. Calder had studied the architecture and scale of the buildings that bordered the site, but had never visited Grand Rapids nor seen the site firsthand.

ALEXANDER CALDER: MOBILE ARTIST, SCULPTOR, AND INNOVATOR

*A*lexander Calder was already a world-renowned artist when he was commissioned to create the first NEA-funded work of public art, *La Grande Vitesse*. Calder was born in 1898 in Lawnton, Pennsylvania into a family of artists. He studied engineering in college and worked at a series of odd jobs before devoting himself to the arts. During the Depression era, Calder created a new form of metal sculpture known as the mobile. At first, the moving parts of his mobiles were operated with cranks and levers, but he later began hanging them so that the shapes danced and spun with currents of air.

In the 1960s, Calder was at the forefront of the new public art movement in America. In addition to *La Grande Vitesse*, his other monumental abstract works from this era include *El Sol Rojo* (The Red Sun), installed in Mexico City for the Summer Olympics in 1968, and *Flamingo*, installed in 1974 in a federal plaza in Chicago with percent-for-art funding. Like *La Grande Vitesse*, *Flamingo* is a brilliant red. Its curved shape rises from the ground like a giant creature awakening. The residents of Chicago celebrated the dedication of *Flamingo* with circus wagons, marching bands, and a hero's welcome for Calder. He died in 1976 at the age of 78.

When Calder's sculpture was unveiled to city residents, most people were puzzled. They complained that it was too big, too expensive, too blindingly red, and too modern. Yet with time, the uproar died down. The citizens of Grand Rapids grew fond of the giant abstract sculpture in their midst. *La Grande Vitesse* became a symbol of pride for the city and eventually appeared on everything from street signs to garbage trucks.

Reaction to other public works by the most famous names in the modern art world followed a similar pattern. At first, people were confused or even hostile toward them, but eventually they learned to accept and even embrace the new works. *Batcolumn*, by Swedish American pop artist Claes Oldenburg, was installed outside a federal building in downtown Chicago in 1977 with funding from a program called Art in Architecture (AiA) and a percent-for-art formula like the one first established during the New Deal. The work is a towering 101-foot-tall (31m) baseball bat that stands on its knob with an open mesh pattern through which the sky and buildings around it are visible. The artist said the work was inspired by Chicago's "verticality"—its stone columns, chimneystacks, construction cranes, and skyscrapers. It is also a salute to baseball, a favorite pastime for many Chicagoans. On the day of its dedication, some city residents complained that *Batcolumn* was an eyesore and a waste of taxpayer money. Yet with time, people grew to like the sculpture and the controversy subsided.

Public Art in the Urban Plaza

Claes Oldenburg's *Batcolumn* of 1977 is a tribute to the skyline of Chicago, Illinois, and the city's love of baseball.

The directors of the new arts programs had another goal in mind when they commissioned artists like Calder and Oldenburg to create giant modern works for urban spaces. Throughout the 1960s and 1970s, U.S. cities were often seen as bleak, claustrophobic places, dominated by high-rise office towers, multi-story parking garages, and concrete plazas.

In a rush to modernize downtown areas, historic buildings and even entire neighborhoods were bulldozed. Cities in this era were also plagued by a host of social problems, including rising crime rates, corruption of local officials, and an outbreak of violent race riots. Many people began to abandon the cities and move to suburbs that were newer, cleaner, and safer. Clearly, there was no quick fix for these complicated social problems, but the hope was that artists could at least make cities more attractive again and help to lure people back.

As part of this city improvement effort, hundreds of abstract sculptures were installed in the middle of concrete plazas surrounded by institutional-looking high-rise buildings. The idea was that these works would add a human dimension to the harsh modern architecture of the city. By the 1970s, this trend had spread throughout the country and many private businesses had also begun to place large abstract sculptures in the plazas around their offices and corporate headquarters. These works became so commonplace that the derogatory term "plop art" was coined to describe public artworks that were plopped down to spruce up cities, without regard to the context, history, or environment of the site. "In this era, public art simply meant placing large-scale works in open plazas, marking them as 'unique' even as the strategy eventually became generic,"[7] explains museum director and author Tom Finkelpearl.

The Controversy over *Tilted Arc*

It would take several high-profile controversies that captured national headlines to change the direction of public art toward works that were a better fit for their surroundings. It is hardly surprising that public art has a "lightning rod tendency" to spark controversy, say art historians, "precisely because it's public and because it's art."[8] The Washington Monument and Statue of Liberty were controversial in their day. The difference was one of intensity, as public artworks became caught up in the culture

wars of the 1970s and 1980s, the bitter cultural battles that raged in the media and the halls of Congress over public morality, elitist attitudes in the art world, government censorship, and free expression.

The stormiest battle over a major work of public art in the twentieth century involved a sculpture called *Tilted Arc*, created by American artist Richard Serra and funded with percent-for-art money through the Art in Architecture program. It was installed in a federal office plaza in New York City in 1981. Serra was celebrated in the art world for enormous Minimalist works that he forged from steel. *Tilted Arc* was a curved 73-ton (66.2t) wall of Cor-Ten steel 102 feet long (31m) and 12 feet high (3.7m) that turned a brownish-rust color when oxidized in the open air. Federal workers in the buildings that surrounded the plaza had not seen Serra's design before the massive work was installed. They complained that *Tilted Arc* cut the plaza in half in a way that seemed threatening, blocked their view, and forced them to detour around it.

Within months of its installation, thirteen hundred office workers had signed petitions demanding the work's removal. A

Federal employees in downtown New York City were very unhappy with Richard Serra's *Tilted Arc* of 1981. The piece was removed and destroyed four years later.

DECIDING THE FATE OF *TILTED ARC*

In May of 1985, art critic Calvin Tomkins recapped the three days of bitter and divisive public hearings that would decide the fate of Richard Serra's sculpture Tilted Arc. *The following are excerpts from his account in the* New Yorker *magazine:*

Fifty-six people spoke against the sculpture, voicing complaints that by this time were well known: that it was ugly; that it spoiled the view; that it prevented the plaza from being used for concerts, performances, or social gatherings; that it attracted graffiti; that it made access to the building difficult. . . .

A hundred and eighteen people rose to defend his sculpture—fellow artists, writers, musicians, museum curators, and public figures. . . .

Relatively few pro-*Arc* speakers defended the sculpture on aesthetic grounds. Some of Serra's most fervent supporters actually dislike the piece, and feel considerable sympathy for the office workers who have to look at it every day. They argued as they did because of the larger issues that seemed to be involved—issues of artistic freedom and the government's role in support for the arts. . . . As [Serra] phrased it, freedom of creative expression implies that once an artist has been selected and commissioned by the government, "the artist's work must be uncensored, respected, and tolerated, although deemed abhorrent, or perceived as challenging, or experienced as threatening.". . .

Even if you feel, though, that the [federal government] made a mistake in commissioning *Tilted Arc* (as I think it did), there is something to be said for the hated monster. In its rough, confrontational way, it has pushed the whole notion of public art—what it is, what it could or should be—into clearer focus for a great many people. It is already a landmark, and it will continue to be one for years to come, even if it goes away.

Calvin Tomkins. "Tilted Arc." *New Yorker*, May 20, 1985, pp. 95–101.

public hearing was convened in 1985 in which the workers were pitted against artists and art critics. The artists defended Serra, not because they particularly liked the sculpture but because they believed it would set a dangerous precedent if *Tilted Arc* were removed and Serra denied his freedom of expression. A panel voted four to one in favor of the workers and ruled that *Tilted Arc* should be relocated. Since no suitable place could be found, the mammoth steel sculpture was cut into pieces and discarded in a scrap metal yard.

At the time the *Tilted Arc* controversy erupted, government support for the arts was already under attack by a vocal group of conservative lawmakers in the U.S. Congress who argued that the NEA and other arts programs channeled taxpayer money to works that were elitist and un-American. Some artists reacted to the threat of censorship by trying to push the boundaries further. They created works for museum shows that were intentionally shocking, obscene or politically provocative. With federal funding for the arts in danger, artists and art sponsors began to reflect on the role of public art in U.S. society and how to balance the expressive rights of artists with their responsibility to the communities where the works were located.

Putting the Public in Public Art

The removal of *Tilted Arc* did not put an end to public art controversies, but it did make it clear that artists could no longer afford to dismiss public opinion. The federal Art in Architecture program revised its guidelines to involve local communities in the selection of artists and sites for their works. For their part, artists began an effort to educate members of the public and seek their input during the design process. There was also a growing awareness that public art was far more successful when it was site-specific, or meaningful to the architecture, history, and environment of the site where it was placed.

In fact, the move toward site-specific public artworks had begun many years earlier, as the federal government's role in commissioning public art began to shrink and local arts groups stepped in. The city of Philadelphia, Pennsylvania, pioneered the nation's first municipal percent-for-art law in 1959. Like the New Deal program, this law required that one percent of all public construction funds in the city be set aside to enhance public buildings and spaces with artwork such as sculpture, murals, mosaics, and fountains. In the next two decades, other cities and states followed by enacting their own percent-for-art laws, among them Baltimore, Maryland; San Francisco, California; Seattle, Washington; New York City; Phoenix, Arizona; Miami, Florida; Kansas City, Missouri; and the entire state of Hawaii. By 1980, all fifty states had their own arts agencies, and public art began to show up in libraries, community centers, fire stations, zoos, and airports and on parks, roadways, and bridges. City officials viewed public art as a vital part of their efforts to revive urban downtowns and neighborhoods. They also saw it as a way for their cities to distinguish themselves at a time when shopping malls, fast food chains, office parks, and even airports had started to look nearly identical from one U.S. city to the next.

Today, public artworks have become more popular than ever before. They are an important part of urban planning projects in many cities, create interesting civic spaces where people can interact, and help restore pride in struggling neighborhoods or entire small towns. "The incorporation of art in our public space helps give expression to our community values," says Kevin Foy, a former mayor of Chapel Hill, North Carolina. "When we encourage art, we also encourage creativity and thoughtfulness."[9]

Public Art in the City

For hundreds of years, public art has been closely identified with cities. Fountains, sculptures, arches, and monuments make city centers, parks, and plazas interesting and distinctive places in which to live and visit. Public artworks such as Michelangelo's giant marble statue of the biblical figure David in Florence, Italy; the Eiffel Tower in Paris, France; the Statue of Liberty in New York City Harbor; and the giant Gateway Arch that frames the midwestern city of St. Louis, Missouri, are instantly recognizable in media images. They brand the cities in which they are found.

Yet public art in U.S. cities faces many challenges. It must compete with the everyday distractions of urban life, including noisy traffic, towering buildings, flashy commercial billboards, unpredictable weather, vandalism, and pollution. One way to create a presence is to be gigantic. The first public works of art to emerge in the 1960s and 1970s were enormous abstract sculptures by famous artists such as Pablo Picasso and Alexander Calder.

Although some went on to become popular city landmarks, it was clear that these artworks could not rescue cities from the overwhelming problems they faced. Giant works of sculpture failed to transform the box-like buildings and stark concrete plazas that resulted from years of modern architecture. Masterworks by celebrated artists had little impact in improving the lives of city residents who faced troubling issues like poverty, crime, unemployment, vandalism, and graffiti. It was also too late to try to restore urban public spaces that had been bought up by private developers to build shopping malls, chain stores, and office parks.

Slowly, the goals for public art began to change. Artists shifted away from works that might be at home in a museum to those that reflected the unique cultural heritage and environment of their sites. The idea was to build civic pride, give cities a renewed sense of character and place, and create memorable spaces for people to come together to enjoy the city or, in some cases, retreat from its busy streets.

As the goals for public art evolved, so, too, did its forms. Towering abstract or Pop Art sculptures still serve as centerpieces, meeting spots, and photo opportunities in many downtown areas, but urban artworks are increasingly built into the infrastructure of the city. They take the form of street furniture, such as park benches, street lamps, bus shelters, and bicycle racks. They appear in subway and train stations or on bridges and highway underpasses, where they enliven the commute from home and work.

Some U.S. cities have also made a strong commitment to integrating public art into the architecture and life of the city. In this approach, sometimes called cultural planning, public art becomes part of a thoughtful, more far-reaching vision to improve the quality of life in the city by reviving downtowns, preserving historic places, sponsoring arts education, and creating art parks where people can gather and interact. It also means learning from the lessons of *Tilted Arc* and ensuring that residents have a voice in decisions about how to create vibrant, livable spaces in which art is a part of their daily lives.

Modern Sculptures as City Centerpieces

At the time the new federal public arts programs of the mid-1960s were getting underway, conditions had grown bleak in many U.S. cities. Towering glass and steel office buildings dominated the skyline, often blocking out the sun. Entire neighborhoods had been torn down to make way for modern construction projects. Middle-class families were abandoning the city in droves for new suburban neighborhoods that they perceived as safer and cleaner.

Arts agencies that aimed to address these problems, such as the NEA's Art in Architecture Program, turned to masters of the art world to create large freestanding modern sculptures for city streets and plazas. The tremendous scale of these works was made possible by the invention of new supersize cranes and manufacturing techniques. The larger the work, the more prestige it was thought to bring to the artist and the host city. Although members of the community were rarely consulted about the placement or design of these works, some artworks became popular city symbols. With time, the citizens of Grand Rapids, for example, learned to appreciate Calder's *La Grande Vitesse* and were proud to have the work of a celebrated modern master in their town.

The second public artwork to be commissioned by the AiPP, *Black Sun*, by Japanese American sculptor, Isamu Noguchi, was a popular success from the outset. Noguchi had started his career by creating stand-alone sculpture on a grand scale, but later began to incorporate elements of landscape design and traditional Japanese gardens in his work. *Black Sun* was installed in Seattle, Washington's Volunteer Park in 1969. It is a giant circle of black granite, 9 feet (2.7m) in diameter, with irregular shapes projecting out from its surface. It is pierced with a large round opening that frames Seattle's landmark Space Needle tower and the majestic Olympic Mountains in the distance. The work heightens the natural beauty of its site, which is why local residents, who fondly call it "The Donut," were quick to embrace it.

In contrast, another Minimalist work by Noguchi, also designed for the city of Seattle, illustrates the pitfalls of public art that is imposed on city residents without their input. *Landscape of Time* was installed in front of a new federal office

Isamu Noguchi created *Black Sun* for Volunteer Park in Seattle, Washington, in 1969. Locals often refer to it as "the doughnut."

building in the city in 1975 with percent-for-art funding. It consists of five minimally-carved pink granite boulders in different shapes and sizes, which were supposed to create a space for quiet reflection. Yet to many viewers, it looked like a random grouping of rocks that seemed out of place in front of an institutional building. The work became the punch line of jokes in the national media when reporters quipped, "We must have rocks in our head."[10] Critics of federal arts sponsorship lashed out, too, asking why the government was "wasting tax dollars on that junk you call art."[11]

Abstract Sculpture That Engages Audiences

In the aftermath of works that were widely perceived as expensive flops, including *Landscape of Time* and *Tilted Arc*, artists have continued to create abstract sculptures for urban public spaces, but the newer works are interactive and engaging. The artist carries out extensive research about the site and designs a work that is made to fit its specific environment and public uses.

One of the new abstract urban sculptures to captivate audiences is *Cloud Gate,* by India-born British artist Anish Kapoor. *Cloud Gate* was designed for the grand opening of an urban art park in Chicago, Illinois, called Millennium Park, built on an abandoned railroad yard and opened to the public in 2004. Affectionately nicknamed "The Bean" by local residents, Kapoor's sculpture is a colossal ellipse or bean-shaped work, made of stainless steel so highly polished that it appears to flow like silvery-white liquid mercury. Like a funhouse mirror, the high-gloss surface casts distorted reflections of the city's dramatic skyline, the park, and people walking by. Underneath the sculpture, crowds gather in a space the size of a small chapel to watch their reflections warp and multiply. Although its massive size and abstract style seem to put *Cloud Gate* in a category with earlier modern works, the way that audiences interact with it marks it as something different.

Janet Echelman's breathtaking aerial works, created from fishing net and steel cables, could not be more different from *Cloud Gate*, but they have a similar impact on audiences. Her giant nets, inspired by forms found in nature such as spider webs and trees bending in the wind, soar high above the urban landscape, sometimes stretching more than 300 feet (91.4m) into the air. She collaborates with engineers, computer scientists, architects, and textile and lighting designers to build and install her complex works, and yet the end result is that they appear to be floating freely, billowing and dancing with currents of air. One of her urban artworks, called *Her Secret is Patience*, installed in a downtown Phoenix, Arizona, park in 2009, is a massive funnel

The polished stainless steel surface of *Cloud Gate* by Anish Kapoor distorts the reflection of onlookers at Millennium Park in Chicago, Illinois.

shape inspired by patterns of desert winds and cactus flowers. During the day, the sun shines through the nets, casting intricate shadows on the ground. At night, colored lights installed beneath the work create a theatrical effect. Echelman explains that the removal of *Tilted Arc* made a deep impression on her. "That sculpture staked out a point on the number line of interacting with the public as an aggressive act," she says. "Instead of blocking your view and pathway, my work colors your view yet allows you to see the world through it."[12]

Whimsical Works of Pop Art

While many viewers found the giant abstract sculptures of the 1960s and 1970s off-putting, they were more likely to be amused by the urban sculptures that grew out of the Pop Art movement of the same era. Pop Art drew its inspiration from American popular culture, advertising, and media images. By taking everyday objects such as clothespins, lipstick, and cheeseburgers as its subject matter, pop art mocked the concept of art

NEW YORK CITY'S ARTS FOR TRANSIT PROGRAM

One of the largest public art collections in the world can be found in a surprising place: beneath the ground in New York City's subway stations. It is estimated that more than 5 million people travel through the city's subway stations on an average weekday. As they enter and exit stations, pass through the turnstiles, and wait on train platforms, they encounter works by some of the most famous artists in the world as well as new and emerging ones. Founded in 1985, the Arts for Transit program was conceived as a way to remedy a system plagued by graffiti-covered subway cars, dim lighting, and stations in disrepair. Arts for Transit sets aside a percentage of subway renovation and rebuilding costs for public art. The works are created from traditional building materials like those used in the original stations, including bronze, steel, mosaic glass, and tile. Among the most popular of the works are odd-looking bronze creatures that climb the stairways or sit with waiting passengers on benches, brightly-colored stained glass mosaics that depict a map of the entire subway system, and a long wall of looping, swirling porcelain tiles in eye-popping colors.

The colorful mural Whirls and Twirls *was designed by Sol LeWitt.*

Clothespin in Centre Square, Philadelphia, Pennsylvania, is one of Claes Oldenburg's first Pop Art sculptures.

that is valued on the market, collected, and sold. The free-spirited founder of the Pop Art movement, Andy Warhol, created paintings and prints of iconic objects and figures such as Campbell's tomato soup cans, Coca-Cola bottles, and larger-than-life celebrities like Marilyn Monroe, often in bright, garish colors. He appropriated the images, meaning that he borrowed and reproduced them over and over again in a new context, until their original meanings were changed.

In its early years, Pop Art in public spaces took the form of enormous stand-alone sculptures of mass-produced consumer items. For viewers, the surprise often came from experiencing familiar objects enlarged to hundreds of times their normal size. More than any other artists, Swedish American sculptor Claes Oldenburg and his wife and artistic collaborator Coosje van Bruggen made gigantic Pop Art works in public spaces their specialty. Their public sculptures of everyday household items include a massive clothespin, button, lipstick, paintbrush, and electric plug, and a cherry on a spoon that also serves as a pedestrian bridge. Oldenburg defended his work from critics who called it lowbrow or unsophisticated, saying that sculpture "has to have the capacity for surprising you and renewing itself and changing in your imagination. When we do a sculpture, we try to load it up with a lot of possible ideas and directions for content."[13]

One of Oldenburg's first and most famous Pop Art sculptures, *Clothespin*, is, as its name suggests, a towering steel clothespin that rises 45 feet (13.7m) into the air in the center of Philadelphia, Pennsylvania. On the surface, everyone agrees that it is an oversized household item. Some also see it as a nostalgic symbol of domestic life at a time when people hung their wash to dry; others call it a mocking commentary on politics in the city. Since it stands directly across from the city hall, a cartoonist joked in the local newspaper that it should support an invisible clothesline where politicians can hang their "dirty linen." For those with insider knowledge of the Philadelphia art scene, the two separate pieces of the clothespin also mimic a lover's kiss, a clever nod to one of the most famous abstract sculptures in the Philadelphia Museum of Art, *The Kiss*, by Romanian sculptor Constantin Brâncusi.

In recent years, works like Oldenburg's *Clothespin* that recreate everyday household items have inspired sculptures of other familiar objects and figures blown up to enormous scale or portrayed in surprising ways, including comic book-style figures, fanciful and shiny balloon animals, robots, mythical creatures, cars, and celebrities. These are sometimes grouped loosely together under the term *Neo-Pop*. One popular piece in Denver, Colorado, *I See What You Mean*, by multimedia artist and sculptor Lawrence Argent, greets visitors to the Denver Convention Center. It is a giant, 40-foot-tall (12.2m) sculpture of a bear standing on its hind legs, painted in brash neon blue. The bear's oversized nose and paws are pressed up against the large glass windows of the upper floors of the convention center building. The effect is comic and a little unsettling as the bear peers curiously at the people inside, even as they gaze out at it.

Building Community Pride with Murals

Unlike other forms of urban public art to emerge in the 1960s, such as abstract and Pop Art sculpture, mural painting was a community-based movement from the start. It evolved as a way of raising ethnic and racial consciousness in some of the poorest, most neglected urban neighborhoods in the country. In many cases, artists worked alongside community members in the

THE BIRTH OF ROCK & ROLL

FOREBEARERS OF CIVIL RIGHTS

The Great Wall of Los Angeles, one of the longest murals in the world, is painted onto the concrete walls of the Tujunga Wash, a part of the large system of drainage aqueducts in southern California.

design and painting of the murals. Once a mural went up, other improvements often followed. Residents gained a newfound sense of pride in their neighborhoods. They picked up trash, planted gardens, organized community events, and reclaimed their streets from drug dealers.

The urban muralists of the 1960s and 1970s often drew their inspiration from the great Mexican mural painters of the 1920s, sometimes called "the big three": Diego Rivera, David Alfaro Siqueiros, and José Clemente Orozco. These painters covered the walls of public buildings in their native land with heroic folk art–style paintings in bright colors that featured themes from Aztec history, Catholicism, and folk legend. The murals were meant to appeal to illiterate peasants and residents of Mexico City's desperately poor urban slums.

In the United States, the mural revival began as a grass-roots protest movement during the years of the civil rights struggle. As the movement spread, city officials began to realize the potential of community murals to improve the quality of life in urban neighborhoods. They developed their own

JUDY BACA: MURALIST, EDUCATOR, SOCIAL ACTIVIST

It is hard to separate Judy Baca's mural painting from her work as educator and social activist. Since she began creating murals in the 1970s, she has been deeply committed to community-based public art. Born in 1946 in a Chicano (Mexican American) neighborhood of Los Angeles, California, she was raised by her mother, who worked in a tire factory, and her grandmother, a Mexican herbal healer. For her first community mural project in a local park, she recruited members of rival Chicano gangs to assist with the painting and was forced to post lookouts to prevent fellow gang members and police from interfering. Her most ambitious mural, the *Great Wall of Los Angeles*, was completed in 1984 after seven years of fundraising, designing, and painting. The project involved more than four hundred ethnically-diverse young people, many of whom had served time in the juvenile justice system, as well as other artists, historians, and community members. Baca has painted murals on the walls of schools, theaters, prisons, recreation centers, airports, and hospitals. She has also worked to develop new digital technologies for creating and restoring murals in public spaces. "I want to use public space to create a public voice, and a public consciousness about the presence of people who are, in fact, the majority of the population but who are not represented in any visual way," Baca says. "By telling their stories we are giving voice to the voiceless and visualizing the whole of the American story."

Quoted in "Judith F. Baca: Artist, Educator, Scholar/Activist and Community Arts Pioneer," Social and Public Art Resource Center (SPARC). www.sparcmurals.org.

mural-painting programs or granted permission for artists to organize communities and paint on urban spaces. Los Angeles and Philadelphia, in particular, developed large-scale mural arts programs under the leadership of two dynamic female artists. Judy Baca led the mural movement in Los Angeles. She combined her artwork with social activism focused on improving the lives of poor urban youth and migrant farm workers. Through her nonprofit group, the Social and Public Art Resource Center (SPARC), she created murals throughout California and the Southwest and mentored hundreds of young people, whom she trained to assist in the design and painting. One of her most ambitious works, the *Great Wall of Los Angeles*, completed in 1984, stretches for an entire half mile (.8 km) just outside of Los Angeles along a flood control channel (a channel below street level that collects water and prevents flooding). In a series of bold, vibrantly-colored panels that read like a people's history of the state of California, the *Great Wall of Los Angeles* depicts the role of ethnic and racial minorities in events such as the California Gold Rush, the building of the transcontinental railroad, and the civil rights struggle.

A similar mural program in Philadelphia got its start in the 1970s as a way to combat a growing problem of graffiti and urban blight (the decay of a city area because of neglect, crime, or lack of economic support). Graffiti artists, called taggers, were defacing walls, buses, billboards, and private property, often working in the stealth of night with their aerosol spray cans and brushes. Fed up with spending thousands of dollars to scrub and whitewash city property, officials reached out to the tagger gangs and offered them a deal. If they signed a pledge not to engage in illegal activity, they would be free from prosecution for any prior acts of vandalism. They would also be paid to take part in a citywide mural movement. Artist Jane Golden became part of the program in the 1980s. She hired professional artists, expanded the training opportunities for urban youth, and turned Philadelphia's mural arts program into the most successful of its kind in the country. Since the 1980s, more than two thousand murals have been painted in neighborhoods throughout the city. In vibrant colors and styles, they depict local heroes, historic figures, symbols of ethnic pride, and realistic and imaginary landscapes.

Public Art Disguised as Urban Infrastructure

Murals and giant sculptures stand out and attract the attention of passersby. In contrast, some public art becomes part of the infrastructure of the city: its roads, walkways, subway stations, park benches, lampposts, and bus shelters. For artists, the form or shape of the piece often follows from its function. A movement to include functional public art in city parks and plazas gained popularity in the late 1970s.

At first, the emphasis of the functional art movement was on works that blended seamlessly into the urban environment. Street furniture such as benches, tables, and streetlamps had a spare, Minimalist style. One of the best-known artists practicing in this style, Scott Burton, created park benches, tables, and other urban amenities out of roughhewn blocks of granite. He wanted his works to disappear into the site so that they would barely be perceived as art. In his view, art should "place itself not in front of, but around, behind, underneath (literally) the audience."[14]

In recent years, the understated, Minimalist style practiced by artists like Burton has been replaced by a very different aesthetic. Artists continue to create works of street furniture for public spaces, but these often have a creative, whimsical flair that captures people's attention, rather than hiding from it. These artworks also tell compelling stories about the history and culture of the places where they are found. They include bicycle racks in the Wall Street financial district of New York City shaped like dollar signs, cast-iron tree guards

The sculptural bike rack *The Wall Street* is one of nine designed by David Byrne in collaboration with the Public Transit Authority of New York City in 2008.

CARE AND MAINTENANCE OF PUBLIC ART

The condition of outdoor public art is an international problem. Car exhaust, smog, the wear and tear of weather, vandalism, graffiti, birds, and the occasional reckless driver threaten to erode and destroy public monuments and artworks in cities around the world. Restoring these works involves power washing, scrubbing, waxing, and polishing. Sometimes cities must hire art conservation experts to determine how best to deepen the fading colors on a wall mural or apply a protective coating to bronze or steel sculptures. In some cases, responsibility for maintaining public works of art falls to city parks departments. In others, percent-for-art funding includes some money for maintenance. Yet these local funding sources often grow unreliable when budgets are tight.

Since it is difficult to attract business and tourism dollars if artworks fall into disrepair, city leaders have gotten creative in their efforts to protect public art. A program in San Francisco called Art Care appeals to private donors to pay for repairs to aging public sculptures. A similar program in Boston, Massachusetts, Adopt a Statue, is an effort to enlist private citizens and corporations to protect favorite works. The city of Carbondale, Colorado, has experimented with another way to pay for maintenance. For four weeks in 2010, all of the public artworks in town were concealed under black plastic and wrapped with caution tape. As financial contributions were received, the plastic was removed and the artworks came out of hiding.

in Louisville, Kentucky, that mimic the traditional carved walking sticks made by local craftsmen, and stools in the Fashion District of Los Angeles shaped like brightly colored spools of thread.

Public art also adds character and vitality to once sterile and industrial-looking highways, electric stations, water treatment plants, and other large-scale urban infrastructure projects. In a unique collaboration with city planners and engineers, artist Marilyn Zwak was commissioned to create an art installation for a new six-lane highway in Phoenix, Arizona. The highway was controversial because its planned path threatened to divide neighborhoods and destroy homes. As a way of giving something back to the community, city leaders proposed using local percent-for-art money to create artwork along the highway. Zwak's site-specific work, *Our Shared Environment,* includes thirty-four murals sculpted from adobe, the native clay, that wrap the walls alongside the highway. These represent lizards, cacti, and other desert plants, as well as patterns recreated from shards of American Indian pottery that were unearthed by archeologists before construction on the highway began.

Art with a Local Sensibility

In recent years, works of public art that convey a strong sense of place, like the Phoenix highway project, have been built in city centers and urban art parks. They greet visitors arriving at airports, walking along urban rivers and coastal waterways, exploring historic neighborhoods, or descending to the platforms of a train station.

One of the earliest and most successful examples of urban public art with a distinctive local sensibility serves as a gateway to the city of Cincinnati, Ohio. Artist Andrew Leicester won a national competition to create a major work in honor of the two-hundredth anniversary of the city in 1988. His *Cincinnati Gateway* stands at the official entrance to a renovated park along a once heavily polluted riverfront. It incorporates references to Cincinnati's past, including canal locks and steamship stacks, which reflect the city's history as a thriving river-trading port, and flying pigs, symbols of its nineteenth-century role as a hog butchering capital. (One of the city's nicknames is "Porkopolis," which was an embarrassment to city leaders who fought unsuccessfully to have the pigs removed from the design.) The main feature of *Cincinnati Gateway* is an earthen mound 250 yards long (229m), constructed to resemble an effigy mound like those used by ancient American Indian tribes of the region for ceremonial rites. On the top of the mound, the Ohio Riverwalk follows a winding course along the river and crosses a suspension bridge with tall pillars that extend upward through the gaping mouths of fanciful sculpted fish. At the top of the cables are the winged pigs, which have become one of the most popular features of the work.

In its conception and design, *Cincinnati Gateway* represents a break from the urban public art of the past. It draws inspiration directly from the culture and environment of its site. Unlike giant sculptures that were "plopped down" in urban plazas, works like *Cincinnati Gateway* become a vital part of the life and architecture of the city.

3

A New Way of Remembering the Past

Monuments and memorials are a unique and powerful form of public art. They are built to pay tribute to events and heroes of the past, but are often hotly debated in the present because they reflect contemporary values about how and what to remember. (The words "monument" and "memorial" are often used interchangeably, but a monument usually commemorates great heroes and moments in history, while a memorial pays tribute to the dead.) Throughout history, monuments and memorials have celebrated the military might of conquering nations, honored the dead, and sung the praises of heroes, patriots, gods, and prophets. More recently, they have also brought people together to mourn and heal after tragic events or to bear witness to shameful episodes in history.

Monuments shape the way people remember the past, but they also have tremendous power to sway emotions in the present. The ruthless totalitarian dictators of the mid-twentieth century, Adolf Hitler in Nazi Germany, Joseph Stalin in the Soviet Union, and Mao Zedong, the communist dictator who rose to power in China in 1949, built monuments on an epic scale to inspire loyalty and strike fear into those who dared to question their authority. U.S. military leaders, too, have long understood the symbolic importance of monuments. When the United States and its allies invaded Germany at the end of World War II, they ordered all monuments to the Nazi regime destroyed within eighteen months. Decades later, when U.S. troops invaded Iraq in 2003, they toppled and destroyed monuments to the country's brutal dictator, Saddam Hussein, as if to symbolically erase his authority from the map.

A New Wave of Monument Building

In America, the first great wave of monument building started after the Civil War in the 1870s and lasted into the 1920s. The Civil War divided fellow citizens and came perilously close to destroying the nation. In its wake, America was gripped by "monument fever." Cities from coast to coast acquired statues of noble heroes in the classical Greek and Roman style. These were meant to inspire people to rally around the nation and follow in the footsteps of great men, but there were so many bronze and marble statues of inventors, explorers, patriots, statesmen, and generals on horseback that it became hard to tell them apart.

The second major wave of monument and memorial building began in the 1980s and has continued to the present day. Yet the monuments built in recent decades represent a different and more complicated way of remembering the past. Many challenge the traditional myths of American history by paying tribute to people whose contributions were overlooked by previous generations of monument builders. Others commemorate wars, acts of terrorism, and genocide that did not end in decisive victory or glory for the nation. In this crowded monument landscape, there is no longer one style that dominates. Statues built in a classical, heroic, or realist style often stand alongside more somber works composed of Minimalist, abstract forms. So many different monuments crowd the landscape today that some historians warn the country may experience a backlash similar to that of the early twentieth century, when the large number of new public monuments came to be seen "as a worrisome problem of irrational emotional zeal and material excess."[15]

The Vietnam Veterans Memorial

In the United States, the revival of public monument building began with a simple and elegant abstract design for a war memorial on the National Mall in Washington, D.C. In 1981, a young architecture student named Maya Lin was announced the winner of a national competition to design a memorial to honor the U.S. soldiers who died in the Vietnam War. Her winning design, selected from among more than fourteen hundred entries, was radically different from anything that preceded it. Its simple lines and Minimalist, abstract style changed the way that Americans interact with their memorials and set the tone for many later works of public art that commemorate painful events in the nation's history.

The Vietnam Veterans Memorial, seen here in 1982 right before it opened to the public, has the name of every U.S. soldier lost in the war engraved in its stone walls.

MAYA LIN

In 1981, Maya Lin was a twenty-one-year-old architecture student at Yale University when she won the design competition for the Vietnam Veterans Memorial. The following are excerpts from a 1996 interview with Lin.

No matter how public my work gets, it remains intimate, one-on-one with the individual. Even though I use text, I never use text like a billboard, which a hundred people can read collectively. The way you read a book is a very intimate experience and my works are like books in public areas. I think that is what has always made people respond to my work in a very quiet way. . . . In Washington, where there was already a lot of controversy around the Vietnam Veterans Memorial, things just exploded after an article in the Washington Post. The headline read, 'An Asian Memorial for an Asian War.' . . . When I looked at the title of this article, I thought, 'We're in trouble now.' Of course, the veterans were already hearing that I was going to give them a 'ditch,' and now all of a sudden the race issue came right into play. They didn't see the memorial in terms of the inward-looking nature of my works. I stayed very quiet about my political beliefs through the whole public discussion of the Vietnam Veterans Memorial. Obviously I built a memorial that asked us to accept death as the primary cost of war. The minute the piece was opened to the public, the controversy ceased, and I started getting the most amazing letters from veterans.

Quoted in Tom Finkelpearl. *Dialogues in Public Art.* Cambridge: Massachusetts Institute of Technology Press, 2001, p. 118 and 121.

Before the Vietnam Veterans Memorial (the VVM), most war memorials celebrated glory in battle and recognized the noble self-sacrifice of the soldiers who fought and died. The Vietnam Veterans Memorial was a new kind of memorial designed to commemorate a different kind of war. It asked Americans to accept the loss of thousands of lives as the horrible cost of a war that left many people feeling torn about the country's involvement. The United States entered the Vietnam War at a time of heightened anxiety about the spread of communism. U.S. troops joined forces with the South Vietnamese to stop the government of North Vietnam from unifying the country under communist rule. The war was waged in the hot, damp jungles and rice paddies of Southeast Asia in a style of fierce guerilla warfare that American soldiers had never experienced before. The country entered into the war gradually, with the first U.S. soldier killed in 1956. The war effort intensified under President John F. Kennedy and later under Lyndon B. Johnson, who greatly expanded the draft and committed more than half a million U.S. soldiers at the war's peak in 1968. In 1975, with no victory in sight, the last troops arrived home under President Richard M. Nixon. The war also took a heavy toll on the home front. As Americans watched the somber television coverage of body bags arriving on U.S. shores, entire villages burned to the ground, and innocent civilians dead and wounded, public opposition to the war mounted. Protests on college campuses, on the National Mall, and in cities around the country often erupted in violence.

Lin's memorial does not glorify this costly and divisive war. Instead, it concentrates on reflection and healing. The design is composed of two walls of polished black granite buried beneath the ground of the National Mall, which meet in a V shape and taper off at each end. The names of the dead and missing in action are carved in simple letters in order of the year they were killed. Visitors gradually descend deeper below the earth to file past the list of names and reflect on the death of more than fifty-eight thousand American soldiers, before ascending back into the light on the other side. The campaign to build the memorial originated with veterans, who also raised the private funds to make it happen. On the day of its dedication in 1982, thousands of veterans and their families made a pilgrimage to leave personal mementos, flowers, poems, notes, photos, and medals. They traced the soldiers' names with their fingers or stopped to take etchings of the names of friends or loved ones. "I didn't want a static object that people would just look at, but something they could relate to as on a journey, or a passage," Lin explained. "I had an impulse to cut open the earth, an initial violence that in time would heal."[16]

A Black Gash of Shame

Despite the outpouring of emotion at the dedication ceremony, Lin's design for a new type of public war memorial was steeped in controversy. Critics referred to it as "a black gash of shame" and claimed it dishonored the soldiers who fought and lost their lives. Some people were upset by the abstract design, which they complained was elitist and hard to comprehend.

As forces opposed to the memorial grew stronger, they threatened to block its opening. A compromise was finally reached

The Three Soldiers by Frederick Hart was installed near the original Vietnam Veterans Memorial in 1984, as a compromise with critics who demanded a more traditional design.

when Congress approved construction of a more traditional monument within 100 feet (30.5m) of the VVM. *The Three Soldiers*, by sculptor Frederick Hart, is composed of three life-size bronze figures of Vietnam-era soldiers portrayed in a figurative, or realist, style. It was installed in 1984, two years after the dedication of the VVM. In 1993, a second realist sculpture to honor the nurses who served in Vietnam was also added near the site.

Yet it is Lin's monument that has proved to have the far greater impact. From the moment the VVM was opened to the public, the controversy that swirled around its construction all but disappeared. Veterans and their families spoke movingly of the black granite wall as a place of healing and closure. For many soldiers who were greeted with angry antiwar protests when they arrived home from combat, it was a place where they could reclaim their pride and honor in service to their country. Unlike other monuments on the National Mall, there are no steep steps to climb, which makes it accessible to wounded veterans, many of whom arrive in wheelchairs or on crutches. The VVM has become one of the most frequently visited memorials in the country. "No single work since the Washington Monument has done more to change the direction of the memorial landscape,"[17] says historian Kirk Savage.

Never Again: Memorials to the Holocaust

The influence of Maya Lin's abstract, Minimalist design is clear in many recent memorials to the Holocaust, which also create an interactive space through which visitors must physically pass so that they will bear witness to the unimaginable suffering and horror. The Holocaust, the state-sponsored murder of minority groups in Europe by the Nazis and their collaborators from 1933 to 1945, claimed more than 11 million victims, about 6 million of them Jews. The Nazis also killed millions of Gypsies, Poles, homosexuals, Jehovah's Witnesses, Soviet prisoners of war, and people with physical disabilities.

A War Memorial to the Greatest Generation

*A*fter the dedication of the Vietnam Veterans Memorial in 1982, veterans who had fought in previous American wars wondered why they, too, had not been recognized on the National Mall. The National World War II Memorial, dedicated in 2004, honors the 16 million Americans who served in the U.S. armed forces during World War II and the more than 400,000 who lost their lives. To celebrate the brave men often called the "greatest generation," architect Friedrich St. Florian designed a memorial that is everything the VVM is not. White instead of black, it has a classical, grand form. Giant pillars and triumphal arches overflow with laurel wreaths, eagles, and quotes from famous military leaders. Whereas the VVM is quiet and reflective, the World War II memorial is loud with the sound of rushing water fountains. A freedom wall displays a gold star for every hundred soldiers who died in battle, but it is out of reach to visitors. The most controversial aspect of the memorial is its site. It creates a barrier between the Lincoln and Washington Monuments, in an area where crowds used to gather to demand civil rights and protest the Vietnam War. The National World War II Memorial was constructed in the months following the September 11, 2001, terrorist attacks, at a time when Americans felt especially vulnerable. Its bold, imperial forms make a strong statement about the strength and military might of the nation. Critics have compared it to what the Nazis and other enemy powers during the war might have built.

In the early years after World War II, as the atrocities of the Holocaust came to light, artists found it difficult, if not impossible, to conceive of a form of public memorial to express the massive scale of the ugliness and horror. In 1958, the Polish gov-

ernment held a design competition for a permanent memorial at the site of the largest Nazi concentration camp, Auschwitz-Birkenau, where close to a million Jews and hundreds of thousands of other innocent victims had been killed, many of them gassed to death and their bodies burned in crematoriums. Renowned British sculptor Henry Moore served as chair of the jury. "Is it in fact possible to create a work of art that can express the emotions engendered by Auschwitz?" he wondered. "It is my conviction that a very great sculptor, a new Michelangelo or a new Rodin, might conceivably have achieved this."[18] More than four hundred design proposals were submitted for the competition, but Moore and his fellow jurors rejected them all.

Yet as time elapsed and the events of the Holocaust grew more remote, survivors and their families began to search for meaningful ways to ensure that future generations would never again allow such atrocities to occur. "Never again" became the survivors' urgent and anguished plea to the world. Although the Holocaust did not take place on American soil, many survivors who settled in the United States after the war longed for

The National World War II Memorial occupies 7.4 acres (30,000m²) in the Washington, D.C., mall between the Washington Monument and the Lincoln Memorial.

communal spaces in which to memorialize the victims and make sure that Americans, too, would remember and bear witness to their stories.

Since the 1980s, Holocaust memorials have been built in cities across the country. These take a variety of forms, from figurative and representational to Minimalist and abstract in the style of the VVM. They all have the disadvantage of being far removed in time and space from the horrors they recall, and therefore lack the immediacy of similar memorials in Europe, where the Nazi mass murders were carried out, or in Israel, which became a Jewish nation and safe haven for Jewish refugees after the experience of the Holocaust.

Artist George Segal's work *The Holocaust,* dedicated in 1982, uses the language of contemporary art to shock and unsettle viewers. Many of Segal's relatives were murdered in concentration camps. *The Holocaust* is set in a beautiful wooded park overlooking San Francisco Bay, within sight of the Golden Gate Bridge. It is a scene composed of eleven ghostly, sculpted white plaster figures with no facial features, which are displayed behind barbed wire. One of the figures is tattered but stand-

The Holocaust in San Francisco, consisting of eleven ghostly plaster figures, was designed by George Segal and dedicated in 1982.

ing, the sole survivor in the scene. The others lie sprawled in a heap on the ground. Some critics suggest that the impact of *The Holocaust* is diminished in the context of the vast and spectacular landscape around it. (In contrast, Segal created a similar work for a museum that many critics described as disturbing and powerful.)

In the years since the VVM was dedicated, many Holocaust memorials in the U.S. have included an immersive, three-dimensional space for viewers to pass through in order to learn through text from historians and eyewitnesses, photos, artifacts, and re-creations. The New England Holocaust Memorial, dedicated in 1995, stands in the center of Boston, Massachusetts, near the Freedom Trail that winds through the city to mark important sites connected to early American history. In this context, says Holocaust scholar James Young, it becomes a way of "understanding what happens when the principles we take for granted in America are absent."[19] The work features six shining glass towers that symbolize the 6 million Jews murdered and the six memorial candles on a *menorah* (a Jewish candelabra). The towers are set on black granite paths that cross over dark chambers carved with the names of the six major Nazi death camps. Smoke rises from charred embers at the bottom of the chambers. Six million numbers are also etched in the glass of the towers to suggest the numbers tattooed on the arms of concentration camp prisoners.

Remembering the Victims of Terror

In recent years, Americans have felt an almost urgent need to build memorials that bring people together to mourn the victims of terrorist attacks. Like recent memorials to the Holocaust, these too, have been heavily influenced by the VVM's Minimalist design. Many artists have come to believe that traditional forms of figurative public art cannot capture the complex emotions that people feel in the wake of traumatic, large-scale acts of violence. Minimalism has become the dominant language of memorials that provide a communal space for grieving and healing. This is not the Minimalism of a giant, imposing wall of steel like *Tilted Arc*, but of granite or marble towers, smooth, polished surfaces, reflective pools, waterfalls, and groves of trees. Often these memorials also include museums on site that aim to educate, so that as tragic events fade from living memory, future generations will continue to bear witness. The forms may be simple, but the memorials themselves have become elaborate, theatrical, and very expensive to build.

The 9/11 Memorial in New York City, which commemorates the most horrific and deadly terrorist attack on U.S. soil, uses many now-familiar Minimalist forms and symbols to convey a wrenching sense of absence and loss. On September 11, 2001, two airplanes hijacked by Islamic terrorists crashed into the Twin Towers of the World Trade Center complex in New York City and killed close to three thousand innocent civilians, including airplane passengers, office workers, firefighters, and other emergency responders. (There were two additional planes in the attack, one of which crashed into the Pentagon in Washington, D.C. and the other into an empty field in western Pennsylvania after passengers resisted.) Within days of the attack, makeshift memorials sprang up in New York City and around the country with shrines, candles, flowers, drawings, and photos of the victims. Yet it would take years before politicians, family members of the victims, survivors, and city planners could reach consensus about a permanent memorial. In the end, they agreed to redevelop parts of the World Trade Center complex as commercial space but to reserve the hallowed ground where the towers had stood for a memorial to the victims.

An international competition was held and a panel of artists and architects, including Maya Lin, were charged with selecting a winning design from among the more than fifty-two hundred proposals submitted. The panel selected a design by Israeli-born architect Michael Arad and landscape architect Peter Walker called *Reflecting Absence*. In 2011, a decade after the attacks occurred, *Reflecting Absence* was finally opened to the public.

The site is a massive 120,000-square-foot space (11,148 sq. m) that also includes an underground museum with artifacts found in the rubble. It is the most expensive memorial in modern American history, funded mainly by private and corporate sponsors.

Reflecting Absence is clearly inspired by Maya Lin's design for the VVM. Visitors walk through a plaza lined with slender white oak trees before arriving at two pools of water located in the exact spots where the Twin Towers once rose. Thirty-foot (9.1m) waterfalls, symbolizing grief, cascade into the pools before descending further into center pits that suggest a sense of absence and loss. The names of the victims are carved on bronze walls that surround the pools. In what has become a ritual at many victim memorials, people take etchings of the names and leave personal notes and mementos.

At the 9/11 Memorial in New York City, designed by architect Michael Arad and landscape architect Peter Walker, two huge reflecting pools and fountains mark the footprints of the two destroyed towers of the World Trade Center.

Monuments to a Shameful Past

In recent years, the monument landscape in America has also expanded to include a new kind of memorial that publicly acknowledges shameful episodes in the nation's history and aims to restore dignity to the victims who suffered or died. This would have been a radical idea in the nineteenth century, and it still sparks controversy today. Many Americans are uncomfortable with the idea that they should feel ashamed or share responsibility for episodes of racial violence and intolerance that occurred before they were born. Yet for the sponsors of these memorials, commemorating the site of a slave burial ground or a violent, racially motivated lynching (a mob killing, often by hanging) leads to a more honest, complete picture of American history and helps the nation move forward and heal.

In the 1990s, Japanese American groups persuaded lawmakers to reserve a space in Washington, D.C., to recognize the forced evacuation and imprisonment of one-hundred-and-twenty thousand Japanese Americans during World War II. Although these civilians had not broken any laws, the nation was at war with Japan, and some people feared that Americans of Japanese heritage might become traitors. President Franklin D. Roosevelt signed an order authorizing their arrest and confinement in internment camps run by the U.S. Justice Department. In 1988, the government finally broke decades of silence about this shameful episode in U.S. history and issued an official apology. The National Japanese American Memorial, dedicated in 2000, is located just north of the U.S. Capitol building. It honors the valor of the thirty-three thousand Japanese American soldiers who fought in World War II and also tells the painful story of those who were forced from their homes and imprisoned illegally in camps. The memorial is designed in the style of a traditional Japanese Zen garden, bordered by cherry trees and a curved granite wall inscribed with the names of the internment camps and quotes from former prisoners. Within the walls, a sculpture by Japanese American artist Nina Akamu portrays two cranes struggling to break free from barbed wire.

PRESIDENTS AND HEROES CAST IN STONE

Ever since the first public monument commissioned by the U.S. government in 1832, in which George Washington appeared bare-chested and draped in a toga, figurative or realistic monuments to presidents and heroes have attracted their share of controversy. The memorial to President Franklin Delano Roosevelt, dedicated in 1997 on the National Mall in Washington, D.C., is a prime example. More than a decade before he was elected president, Roosevelt was stricken with polio and confined to a wheelchair. Yet he went to great lengths to show himself as healthy and strong because he feared that his disability would have a negative impact on his public image. Although it is hard to imagine today, the press corps of the era respected the president's wishes and typically photographed him covered in a cloak or seated behind a desk.

Memorial designer Lawrence Halprin chose to depict Roosevelt as he believed the former president would have wanted to be portrayed, with a cloak hiding signs of his disability.

Yet this upset many people in the disability rights community, for whom Roosevelt is an inspirational figure. They exerted tremendous pressure on lawmakers, and in 2001, Halprin was forced to add a bronze statue at the memorial's entrance in which the wheelchair is clearly visible. Critics were quick to call this the height of political correctness, but, in fact, historians say the entire memorial ignores the president's wishes. FDR never wanted an elaborate memorial. Supreme Court Justice Felix Frankfurter, who served during the Roosevelt era, wrote, "He left plans for only a modest block of stone no bigger than his desk and without any ornamentation."

Quoted in Erika Doss. *Memorial Mania: Public Feeling in America.* Chicago, IL: The University of Chicago Press, 2010, p. 36.

At the Heart of the American Story: Monuments to Slavery

Although it was at the heart of the American story from the beginning, slavery has proven more difficult to memorialize, because it is associated with feelings of humiliation and shame even for many African Americans who are descended from its victims. One of the few public monuments to slavery, the African-American Monument, was dedicated in 2002 in Savannah, Georgia, a city where the slave trade flourished in the eighteenth century. The monument, by local artist Dorothy Spradley, stands along the heavily touristed riverfront facing the site where hundreds of thousands of enslaved Africans disembarked from ships to be bought and sold at the city's barbaric slave market. The monument portrays a modern black family, including a man, woman, and two children, sculpted as life-size, realist bronze figures. They stand close together with chains encircling their feet. The monument's most controversial ele-

U.S. president Barack Obama gives a speech in front of the Lincoln Memorial as part of his inaugural celebration in 2009.

ment is a graphic description of slavery by poet Maya Angelou that is inscribed on its granite pedestal: "We were stolen, sold and bought together from the African Continent. We got on the slave ships together. We lay back to belly in the holds of the slave ships in each other's excrement and urine together, sometimes died together, and our lifeless bodies thrown overboard together."[20] Savannah residents complained that the words were too disturbing. To appease critics, Angelou added a somewhat more hopeful line to her text: "Today, we are standing up together, with faith and even some joy."[21]

Memorials and the Passage of Time

It is unclear what will happen to any of these memorials and monuments as the events and people they commemorate fade from memory, like the heroes on horseback of the nineteenth century. In some cases, they will evolve and their missions will change as they take on new meanings for new generations. A memorial that once helped troubled veterans of war come together to heal, for example, may become a place where Americans learn to understand that war and its impact on history.

The Lincoln Memorial in Washington, D.C. is an example of a public monument that has taken on new significance with the passage of time. It stands in memory of a martyred president who struggled to preserve the nation through a deadly civil war. At the time of its dedication in 1922, the United States was still segregated and black Americans were denied basic rights and opportunities. Decades later, in 1963, that same monument became a powerful symbol of the struggle for civil rights when Martin Luther King Jr. stood on its steps to declare, "I have a dream." The Lincoln Memorial took center stage again in 2009, when the nation's first African American president, Barack Obama, stood on its steps to deliver an inaugural celebration speech. No one at the time the monument was built, including its architect, could have imagined those scenes.

4

Destination
Public Art

People typically experience public art by accident while waiting for a subway train, sitting on a park bench, or walking through a city square, but sometimes, public art itself is the destination. Giant works of Land Art (also called Earth Art) in remote deserts or mountain ranges draw visitors who are willing to travel long distances to experience them. For those who make the journey, they offer solitude and a chance to reflect on the dramatic beauty of nature or, in some cases, a disturbing glimpse at the human role in altering the natural environment.

Other destination public artworks are found closer to home, in cities and small towns. Large-scale temporary public art installations and art festivals transform the urban landscape for a day, a week, or a year. Hundreds or even hundreds of thousands of people come together to experience works in which billowing sheets of fabric are draped over gates in a city park, man-made waterfalls cascade from scaffolding under bridges, or colorful cords are stretched across a rushing river.

Destination art, says museum curator and author Amy Dempsey, "can take you to another dimension and provide insight into another world, time, place or way of thinking." The location and context of the work are an important part of experiencing and understanding it. "It is the art in its particular setting that is your destination."[22]

Monumental Art Built into the Land

Monumental works of Land Art are usually located off of unpaved roads or remote highway exits in deserts, forests, mountainsides, abandoned military bases, ghost towns, or stone quarries. The Land Art movement began in the turmoil of the late 1960s with a handful of artists who longed to break free from the artistic and commercial limitations imposed by the modern art world. They worked in isolated locations, often in the vast, expansive landscapes of the American West in the spirit of frontier cowboys. They were part of a larger trend in this era of artists who experimented with various forms of art-off-the-easel, determined to create works that could not be collected or sold on the art market. The first works of Land Art were immense, Minimalist, and theatrical, carved from the materials of the earth itself, such as rock, soil, sand, and water. They were usually funded by generous private donors or art institutions, and public mainly in the sense that they were built on open or public lands and accessible to anyone willing to make the demanding physical journey to see them. Visitors who made the trek often described the experience in mystical or spiritual terms, as a journey of self-discovery.

Double Negative is one of the first and most famous of the Land Art sculptures, created in 1969 by Michael Heizer, a pioneer of the movement. Heizer was born into a family of anthropologists and geologists and spent time in his childhood visiting the ruins of ancient civilizations, including the pyramids of Egypt and Mexico. In his own work, he wanted to evoke the sense of awe and wonder he had felt walking among these pre-historic sites. *Double Negative* consists of two massive, sloping trenches, 30 feet wide (9.1m) and 50 feet deep (15.2m), carved into the edge of a rocky canyon outside the town of Overton,

Nevada. Heizer used bulldozers and dynamite to blast away the rock, in this case a whopping 240,000 tons of it (217,724t). He cut the two rectangular trenches from the edge of the mesa (a flat-topped hill with steep sides) so that they line up across a large gap. The work is named for the effect created by the two manmade trenches, or empty spaces, which create a "double negative."

Artist Robert Smithson, another of the Land Art pioneers, also saw his work as directly linked to sacred prehistoric sites, including the mysterious animal-and-serpent-shaped effigy mounds of the Midwest that are believed to have been used by ancient American Indian tribes for ceremonial rites. Smithson displaced more than 6,500 tons (5,897t) of dirt and rock to create his masterwork, *Spiral Jetty*, over the course of six days in April 1970. He chose the site, on the northeastern shore of the Great Salt Lake in Utah, because of the dramatic blood-red color of the water, caused by an accumulation of algae, bacteria, and brine shrimp. Smithson took out a lease on the land in the hope that the project would spark a larger movement to reclaim industrial wastelands and turn them into works of art. (The artist died prematurely at the age of 35 when his small plane crashed while he was surveying a remote site in 1973. Years later,

Spiral Jetty, created by Robert Smithson in 1970 in the Great Salt Lake in Utah, is shown in 2002, when water levels dropped enough to make the work visible once again.

a movement began to involve artists in reclaiming environmentally degraded lands.) Seen from the air, *Spiral Jetty* is a long pathway that extends into the water before it coils into a spiral shape. Smithson and his crew excavated the black basalt rock and dirt used to create *Spiral Jetty* from the nearby hillsides and carried it by truckload to the site. They built up the work to a level just above the height of the water so that people could walk out onto the lake to experience it firsthand. Yet they failed to take into account the unusually low water levels at the time, and by 1976, *Spiral Jetty* was completely submerged. For years, most people were familiar with the work only from photographs, until it made a surprising reappearance in 2002, after months of severe drought in Utah. When the work resurfaced, its coiling pathway appeared white with salt and the water around it had a pinkish tint.

Roden Crater: Sculpting a Volcano

One of the most ambitious works of Land Art ever created, artist James Turrell's *Roden Crater*, is a massive naked-eye observatory like those used by prehistoric civilizations to observe the sun, moon, and stars. Turrell is known for art installations in which he manipulates light and space to create optical illusions that change viewers' perceptions. These include works he calls "skyspaces": enclosed spaces in which viewers observe isolated slices of sky through a hole in the roof. He began his epic masterwork *Roden Crater* in 1979 and, decades later, it remains unfinished. *Roden Crater* is a four-hundred-thousand-year-old extinct volcanic crater in the Painted Desert outside of Flagstaff, Arizona, miles from the nearest road. Turrell purchased the land with support from the nonprofit Dia Art Foundation. Within the crater, he has carved out an amphitheater with a bronze staircase leading up to the sky; chambers; tunnels; and platforms for viewing sections of sky and astronomical events. He also plans rooms where visitors will one day spend the night.

RODEN CRATER: A MUSIC OF THE SPHERES IN LIGHT

*A*rtist James Turrell plans to open his Land Art masterpiece, *Roden Crater*, to the public, but after several decades, the man many call a genius and visionary is still striving to create the perfect viewing experience. The crater is set at an elevation of roughly 5,400 feet (1,646m) in a volcanic field near Arizona's Painted Desert and the Grand Canyon. Turrell's goal for the work is to extend his explorations of light and space from the studio to the vast western landscape. He explains his vision in almost mystical terms on the *Roden Crater* website:

> I did not want the work to be a mark upon nature, but I wanted the work to be enfolded in nature in such a way that light from the sun, moon and stars empowered the spaces. . . . I wanted to make spaces that engaged celestial events in light so that the spaces performed a 'music of the spheres' in light. . . . The work I do intensifies the experience of light by isolating it and occluding light from events not looked at. I have selected different portions of the sky and a limited number of events for each of the spaces. This is a reason for the large number of spaces. . . . It is a piece that does not end. It is changed by the action of the sun, the moon, the cloud cover, by the day and the season that you're there, it has visions, qualities and a universe of possibilities.

Quoted in the website *Roden Crater*. http://rodencrater.com/about.

Turrell hopes to evoke a sense of the ancient geologic time and light conditions that existed before humans ever walked the earth. He explains, "I wanted an area where you had a sense of standing on the planet. I wanted an area of exposed geology like the Grand Canyon or the Painted Desert, where you could feel geologic time. Then in this stage set of geologic time, I wanted to make spaces that engaged celestial events in light. . . . "[23] So far, only invited guests and a handful of desert trespassers have experienced Turrell's masterwork firsthand, although the artist plans to open *Roden Crater* to the public once he has perfected the viewing experience.

Earth and Sky Framed, Wrapped, and Revealed

At the same time that the early Land artists were building monumental works into the landscape, other artists began to create destination works in remote locations using manmade materials and forms. These artists looked for ways to accentuate the beauty of nature by framing ocean, sky, sun, moon, or stars in concrete windows, tunnels, and arches; covering the landscape with giant sheets of fabric and then uncovering it to reveal its features again; or capturing the power of lightning, wind, storms, and crashing waves with metal poles, mirrors, and sound tunnels.

Artist Nancy Holt was one of the only women to be part of the early Land Art movement. She was married to *Spiral Jetty* creator Robert Smithson, and continued to work in the vast landscapes of the American West long after his premature death. Holt's background was as a photographer and filmmaker, and she brought this sensibility to her large earthworks. For her renowned work *Sun Tunnels*, completed in 1976 in a desolate region of the Great Basin Desert of Utah, she consulted with astronomers and engineers in order to precisely align four 9-foot-long (2.7m) concrete tunnels in an "x" pattern, so that they would be ideally situated to observe the summer and winter solstices (the days in December and June when the sun appears to reach its lowest and highest altitudes in the sky above the horizon). On those days, the sun on the horizon is framed in the exact center of the tunnels at solar noon. Holt also pierced

Completed in 1976, Nancy Holt's *Sun Tunnels* comprises four concrete tunnels placed precisely to align with the sun on the summer and winter solstices.

holes into the tops of the tunnels that cast patterns of light onto the bottoms corresponding to different constellations of stars. Visitors are often unimpressed when they first approach the work, which looks like a construction site in the middle of an uninhabited desert. It is only when they spend time sitting inside the tunnels and watching the sunlight stream through them that they appreciate the work's stark and dramatic beauty.

One of the most celebrated works of destination Land Art, constructed of manmade materials, requires a three-hour drive from Albuquerque, New Mexico, and an overnight stay in a rustic cabin in the remote high desert. *Lightning Field*, created in 1977 by artist Walter De Maria, consists of an enormous 1-mile-by-0.6 mile grid (1.6km by 1km) of four hundred polished and pointed stainless steel poles set in place so that despite the unevenness of the desert floor their tips are at a precisely uniform height. The dramatic shifting desert light and passing

A PILGRIMAGE TO
THE LIGHTNING FIELDS

Journalist and art critic Blake Gopnik made the overnight pilgrimage to experience Walter De Maria's celebrated work of Land Art The Lightning Field *and wrote the following account:*

A classic path of sagebrush-covered land, set on an empty plateau 7,200 feet [2194.6m] high. A ring of jagged mountains at its edges. . . . And in the middle, 400 lightning rods, custom-made from stainless steel and laid out in a grid that stretches a mile [1.6km] in one direction and a kilometer [0.6 mi] in the other. . . . *Lightning Field* kept me looking and thinking for longer than I've spent with any other work of art, at least all in one stretch. I wandered the site nonstop from afternoon to night of one long summer's day, and then from before dawn to almost noon the next. . . . I admit that I lucked out. There were evening thunderstorms the first day I went, and the mountains all around were bright with lightning . . . there's no doubt the piece looks great by storm light . . . but the best thing about *Lightning Field* is that it seems to work at least as well, or better, by any other kinds of light, at almost any moment that you come across it . . . . The long trip was necessary to the meaning of this art. One way or another, De Maria's piece is clearly about the West, so it's only right that there should be some kind of trek to get you to your destination.

Blake Gopnik. "Shocks and Awe: Mysterious Art in New Mexico." *Washington Post*, August 13, 2009. http://articles.washingtonpost.com/2009-08-13/opinions/36860988_1_art-world-mysterious-art-art-in-new-mexico.

lightning storms reflect and illuminate the poles in sequence across the field. De Maria tried his hand at many types of art in the experimental spirit of the 1960s, including conceptual artworks in which audiences followed step-by-step, handwritten instructions to play a game or carry out a task. He eventually developed a Minimalist aesthetic, and began to work with stainless steel and other metals. For *Lightning Field*, the remoteness of the desert location and even the difficult journey required to reach it were central to his vision. He wanted viewers to spend extended time with the work, across changing weather and light. "The land is not the setting for the work, but a part of the work,"[24] he said.

A Desert Shrine to the Automobile: *Cadillac Ranch*

Some destination public artworks in remote locations seem to have more in common with giant Pop Art sculptures or kitschy roadside attractions than they do with monumental Land Art like *Lightning Field*. Yet they also alter the landscape and offer a new way of looking at familiar sights. One of the most iconic American works of this type was created in 1974 by a group of self-identified countercultural, rebel artists calling themselves the Ant Farm Collective. It was funded by an eccentric Texas billionaire oilman. *Cadillac Ranch* is a humorous shrine to the automobile and America's obsession with cars. It was originally located in a wheat field 8 miles (13km) outside of Amarillo, Texas, and later moved to an open cow pasture 2 miles (3.2km) further west to escape the expanding city limits. *Cadillac Ranch* is composed of ten vintage Cadillacs, arranged in chronological order by model year from 1949 to 1963, with their noses buried in the ground and their tail fins sticking straight up into the air. A reporter who visited the site in 1987 described the work as "surreal" and "like the product of some extraterrestrial event."[25] Over the years, *Cadillac Ranch* has attracted a steady stream of visitors from around the world, who have left their mark by defacing the cars, ripping off pieces as souvenirs, and splattering fluorescent paint all over them until only the battered frames remain. Eventually, the artists themselves began to encourage this kind of irreverent behavior. Every week, visitors cover the cars in a fresh layer of graffiti before discarding their empty spray cans in an overflowing garbage bin at the pasture's entrance.

Environmental Art That Respects the Landscape

Inspired by works like *Spiral Jetty* and *Lightning Field*, contemporary environmental artists continue to create site-specific art installations in which the natural landscape is a canvas. Yet these artists work in a very different spirit than the bulldozing Land Art pioneers. Instead of altering the land with drill rigs and dynamite or displacing tons of dirt and rock, they draw people's attention to the landscape without permanently disrupting it. Some artists use new technologies, theatrical effects, and dramatic lighting, or merge sophisticated science with art to heighten awareness of natural spaces and change people's perception of them. Others rely solely on primitive building tools and natural materials.

Patrick Dougherty created *Natural History* for the Brooklyn Botanical Gardens in 2010. The sculpture weaves saplings together to make dynamic hollow forms that visitors can enter.

Artist Ned Kahn is fascinated with the natural processes of weather, atmospheric physics, and geology. He creates large-scale public sculptures that make the invisible forces of nature appear visible to audiences. His kinetic sculptures are often located in areas with high winds, crashing waves, or water currents, so they can move, reflect, and respond to natural forces. *Slice of Wind*, created in 1996 and located at the University of Colorado, Boulder, consists of ten thousand metal discs that spin freely and reflect light as the wind passes by them. *Mirror Array*, a temporary installation of hundreds of connected tilted mirrors placed on a beach in northern California, revealed shimmering snapshots of the ocean's surface as waves passed under the work, allowing viewers to see the ocean in a new way.

In contrast, North Carolina-based artist Patrick Dougherty creates monumental, site-specific sculptures out of branches, twigs, and tree saplings that are young enough to be manipulated, which he bends and weaves into shapes that resemble giant tumbleweeds and wind gusts. Dougherty studied primitive building techniques and gradually learned to shape the saplings into his complex, twisted sculptures. He has created public art installations in U.S. cities and around the world, for which he collects saplings by the truckload, and crafts them into nests, cocoons, woolly huts that viewers enter through a doorway, and other imaginative creatures and forms. Some of his stick sculptures are woven into the groves of trees or lashed around buildings. Most deteriorate after a year or two in the wild.

One of the best-known environmental artists in the world, British artist Andy Goldsworthy, creates sculptures for museums and public spaces that are designed almost entirely from stones, twigs, logs, icicles, flower petals, and other natural materials he finds at the site. He assembles these with his bare hands, teeth, and tools such as sharp stones or thorns. Some of his works are short-lived and quickly erode or wash away with wind, rain, and snow. As part of the creative process, Goldsworthy documents these works in photographs. Other works built of stones and logs remain stable for longer. *Spire*, which stands in a park overlooking San Francisco Bay, is a massive 100-foot-tall (30.5m) cone with a delicate tip rising at the top. It was assembled from fallen cypress logs found at the site. In contrast to the early Land Artists, Goldsworthy expresses a profound respect for the landscape as he finds it. "There are occasions when I have moved boulders," he says, "but I'm reluctant to, especially ones that have been rooted in place for many years."[26]

The Twenty-First Century's First Great Public Art Event

Some of the most spectacular destination works of public art in recent years have been enormous temporary installations in city parks and other urban spaces that draw crowds to experience them. They often combine Environmental Art and large-scale spectacle. For a period of sixteen days in February 2005, internationally renowned artists Christo and Jeanne-Claude transformed New York City's Central Park with their work *The Gates*. Christo and Jeanne-Claude became art world celebrities

People stroll in New York City's Central Park in February 2005 under portions of *The Gates* art installation by Christo and Jeanne-Claude.

WRAPPING BUILDINGS AND LANDSCAPES

Husband and wife team Christo and Jeanne-Claude became famous for their monumental art installations in which they wrapped, draped, and veiled buildings and landscapes. Christo studied painting and sculpture in his native Bulgaria before escaping the country's oppressive communist regime and moving to France. He met Jeanne-Claude in Paris when he was commissioned to paint her mother's portrait. The couple first made headlines in 1962, when they barricaded a narrow city street in Paris with 240 oil barrels for a work called *Wall of Barrels, Iron Curtain* that brought traffic to a halt for several hours. The work was meant as a protest against the Berlin Wall, which the Soviets had constructed to cordon off communist East Germany from democratic West Germany and prevent people from escaping. In 1964, the artists immigrated to the United States with their young son and settled in New York City. In 1969, they wrapped the Museum of Contemporary Art in Chicago in a greenish-brown tarpaulin held in place with rope. In 1972, they stretched white fabric fencing, supported by steel posts, over 24 miles (39km) of California hills ending at the Pacific Ocean. In 1983, they wrapped eleven small islands off the coast of Florida with pink polypropylene floating fabric. The artists refused to accept commercial sponsors and self-financed their works through the sale of sketches, collages, and scale models.

in the 1970s and 1980s for their massive temporary Land Art installations, in which they wrapped synthetic fabric around coastlines and small islands or suspended it with steel cables over valleys and rivers, and directed the spontaneous opening of thousands of giant umbrellas across vast areas of land. It took twenty-six years to win approval for *The Gates* project and 21 million dollars to assemble and install, money that the artists raised themselves from the sale of collages and sketches of their plans. *The Gates* was billed as "the first great public art event of the 21st century."[27] It consisted of 7503 vinyl gates draped with saffron-orange pleated nylon cloth, installed over 23 miles (37km) of parkland. Christo described it as "a golden river appearing and disappearing through the bare branches of the trees."[28] At the opening ceremony, the city's mayor tore open the Velcro closure to release the first pleated curtain. A team of six hundred workers unfurled the rest. Huge crowds gathered in the park, where they wandered through the gates and mingled with fellow visitors. One enthusiastic reporter declared, "Paths have become like processionals, boulevards decked out as if with flags for a holiday. Everyone is suddenly a dignitary on parade."[29]

Other Large-Scale Art Installations

The Gates was a tremendous success and generated millions of dollars from the sale of books and souvenirs, and from visitors who poured into the city and patronized local businesses. As a result, New York City officials wasted little time before planning another large-scale public art installation. *The New York City Waterfalls,* conceived by Danish-Icelandic artist Olafur Eliasson and opened in the summer of 2008, was another ambitious feat of engineering. It consisted of four towering waterfall sculptures, 90 to 120 feet tall (27.4m to 36.6m), their frameworks built from metal scaffolding, placed in different locations underneath bridges in the city's East River. Pumps placed at the sites sucked up water from the river and lifted it ten stories into the air to troughs before sending thirty-five hundred gallons per minute cascading back down into the river below. Illuminated by LED lights, the waterfalls created a particularly dramatic spectacle at night. The artist hoped that the work would heighten people's awareness of the rivers and waterways all around them.

One of four man-made *New York City Waterfalls* created by Olafur Eliasson in 2008 sits beneath one of the massive towers of the Brooklyn Bridge.

While few U.S. cities have the resources to produce installations on the enormous scale of *The New York City Waterfalls* or *The Gates*, many have sponsored temporary public art installations that draw residents to familiar landscapes and change the way they think about them. In some cases, these are as simple as a work in Kansas City, Missouri, called *Float* that featured large hammocks arranged in rows on a lawn space in front of the city's convention center. The idea was to break down barriers and allow people to interact in a more relaxed setting while they lay swinging in the hammocks. Other installations are more complicated. In 2012, the city of Pawtucket, Rhode Island, with a population of seventy thousand residents, became the site of "the first river that was ever woven in the United States."[30] Pawtucket was the home of the nation's first successful nineteenth-century textile mill. In a reference to the once-flourishing mill, sculptor Donald Gerola stretched thousands of feet of brightly colored synthetic fabric cords across the rushing Blackstone River for a work he called *Weaving the Blackstone*. He suspended the cords at different heights from 3 feet (.91m) to 36 feet (11m) above the water and wove them through several oversized heddles (the part of a loom where the threads pass). It took two archers with high-powered bows that are normally used to hunt bear to shoot the cords from one side of the river to the other.

From synthetic cords stretched over a river to a giant spiral jetty extending into a lake, destination artworks share in common the ability to draw people to a physical place and change their perceptions of it. Whether they require a journey over difficult terrain or a trip across the city, these artworks achieve their impact by heightening awareness of the environment and making familiar landscapes seem unfamiliar by framing them in a new way.

5

Public Art with a Social Message

$\mathcal{A}$rt in the public sphere, on city streets and buildings where it is hard to ignore, can become a powerful and highly visible form of protest art, a rallying cry for social action, or a means of raising awareness about the excesses of consumerism, environmental issues, poverty, racism, or intolerance. Public art with a social or political message is sometimes official, sponsored by arts groups or sanctioned by government agencies, and at other times unofficial, created by grassroots community groups or individual artists, who often work in stealth to deliver their messages to the streets. By nature, these works are controversial, but they are also often temporary, which gives artists more freedom to make bold statements and take greater risks.

In recent decades, socially conscious public art has witnessed an explosion of forms and styles—from large-scale community-based protest murals to environmental installations to participatory works in which audiences help to shape the final product. The artists who create these works share the belief that public art has the power to bring about change. At their most provocative, they test the limits of artistic free expression and the U.S. Constitution's First Amendment guarantee of freedom of speech. "These artists do not wait for others to realize their ideas," says Anne Pasternak, director of Creative Time, an arts group that sponsors edgy political works. "They do it on their own, investing in deep research, building relationships with community residents, initiating fresh partnerships, sharing their passions, and bravely reclaiming the public domain as a place for creativity and free expression."[31]

Public Art as Social Protest

Today's socially conscious public art has its roots in earlier art forms, including graffiti tagging, community mural painting, and many of the art-off-the-easel forms to emerge in the 1960s. These include Conceptual Art, in which the idea or concept of the work and the process of creating it takes precedence over its aesthetic values, and Installation Art, in which artists transform a space with objects, sound, and lighting to create a three-dimensional experience for viewers. While some of the socially conscious artists of the 1960s and 1970s went to extremes to shock and provoke audiences, others confronted important issues. They denounced the war in Vietnam or called attention to racial or gender discrimination.

Decades later, even as public art has entered the mainstream, many artists continue to create murals, sculpture, and large-scale art installations as a form of social or political protest. Artist Jenny Holzer's signature works are text-based installations that tackle issues such as violence, oppression, and sexist attitudes. Holzer first emerged on the art scene in the early 1980s with a project she called *Truisms* in which she pasted posters on the sides of buildings with pithy one-line phrases, such as "Abuse of power comes as no surprise," and "Everyone's work is equally important."[32] She later displayed her mottos and phrases on electronic billboards, T-shirts, plaques, movie marquees, and even the side of the Goodyear Blimp.

Holzer's most renowned public works are visually arresting light displays in which her text is projected in supersize typeface onto the facades of public buildings or displayed scrolling

In the 2005 series *For the City*, Jenny Holzer projected messages on New York City buildings, such as 30 Rockefeller Plaza.

and blinking across thin strips of screen. In a work called *For the City*, created in 2005, she projected her messages at nighttime onto several landmark New York City buildings. On one night, the text included verses by celebrated poets such as Walt Whitman; on another night, excerpts from declassified U.S. government documents in which words and sentences had been redacted (censored and blacked out) to protect top-secret information. These documents related to the 9/11 terrorist attacks and government interrogations of U.S. soldiers who had tortured and abused prisoners during the Iraq war of 2003–2012. Holzer's work shows how language can be used or manipulated to educate, enlighten, offer comfort, or, sometimes, to twist or conceal the truth.

Whereas Holzer's public works are crafted almost entirely from words, Polish-born American artist Krzysztof Wodiczko (pronounced Vodeeshko) is known for socially conscious light and sound installations that feature visual images. Using industrial-size projectors and loudspeakers mounted on flatbed trucks and scaffolding, he projects his otherworldly video images onto the facades of buildings and monuments in cities around the world. Wodiczko was born in Warsaw, Poland, in the midst of World War II, during the Nazi occupation of his homeland. He spent his childhood in the oppressive post-war years, when Poland was under the Soviet Union's communist rule. As a result of his background, Wodiczko is keenly aware of how governments can abuse power to silence or repress people. His public art often focuses on the trauma and brutality of war and also seeks to shed light on the problems faced by downtrodden, oppressed groups such as undocumented immigrants or the homeless, whose voices are seldom heard.

In one public installation in 2012, *Abraham Lincoln: War Veteran Projection*, Wodiczko spent months interviewing U.S. veterans who had recently returned from the wars in Iraq and Afghanistan about their wartime experiences and the toll their service had taken on their family lives. He then cast video images of the veterans onto a stone statue of Abraham Lincoln in a New York City park, so that they seemed to inhabit the statue and make it come alive. While their testimonies were playing over loudspeakers, their faces were projected onto Lincoln's face, their hands superimposed onto his stone hands. Wodiczko chose the site for its symbolic importance. The Lincoln statue was commissioned several years after the end of the Civil War, the deadliest war in American history. For the artist, this was an ideal location to engage the public in dialogue about the heavy burdens of war. He also hoped that his work would provide a healing place for veterans. Wodiczko explained, "When they come here I hope they will see themselves speaking to the world and to the public, and this will really give them more confidence, more power, and also recognition of the truth of their experience."[33]

The Chicano Murals: A People's Art Movement

In some cases, public works of protest art begin with members of oppressed or marginalized communities themselves, striving for ways to make their voices and issues heard. In the midst of the struggle for civil rights, large-scale community murals emerged as a way for ethnic and racial minority groups to affirm their cultural identity and command the respect and recognition of the larger American public. The mural projects of this era, part of a People's Art movement, were grassroots efforts, led by local artists who worked without outside support from government agencies, corporations, or private donors.

The People's Art movement began with a mural featuring portraits of black heroes from U.S. history, painted on a wall in the gritty, crime-ridden streets of Chicago's South Side, where poor African American residents were caught up in the struggle for civil rights. It later spread to Chicano (Mexican American) communities in California, Texas, Arizona, and New Mexico, where a separate struggle for civil rights, referred to as *El Movimiento* (Spanish for "The Movement"), was also gathering strength. The greatest example of Chicano murals from this era adorns the structural supports of a curving, blue steel bridge that spans a beautiful bay in San Diego, California. The Coronado Bridge was constructed in 1967 to connect the city to the barrier island of Coronado. The murals are located in Chicano Park, a small community park in a neighborhood called Barrio Logan that sits underneath the heavily trafficked bridge and the maze of freeway overpasses that feed into it.

THE *WALL OF RESPECT*

The first documented U.S. mural of the People's Art movement was called the *Wall of Respect*. It was painted on the façade of an abandoned building in a poor, crime-ridden neighborhood on the South Side of Chicago in 1967, at the turbulent height of the Black Power movement. This movement, which focused on racial pride and the founding of separate Afro-centric cultural institutions, captured the imagination of many black artists, writers, politicians, athletes, and academics. The *Wall of Respect* was the vision of a group of Chicago-based artists, who paid for their own paints and materials out of pocket. At the time, images of African Americans were conspicuously absent from most mainstream media, history textbooks, and museums. The artists chose the theme "Black Heroes," hoping that the figures they portrayed would be seen as positive role models that would spur the community to social action. They painted more than fifty portraits of musicians, athletes, actors, writers, religious leaders, statesmen, and activists. When it was completed, the mural became a gathering place for rallies in support of civil rights and for street festivals with arts, music, and poetry readings.

Eventually, the *Wall of Respect* attracted national media attention and sparked a movement that spread to other cities around the country. In 1971, a suspicious fire broke out in the building next door to the mural, and the *Wall of Respect* was destroyed. "I don't think we fully realized the impact it would make," explains mural creator Bill Walker. "It focused on heroes who had stood in the face of controversy. The community as a whole could relate to that."

Quoted in Jeff Huebner. "The Man Behind the Wall." *Chicago Reader*, August 28, 1997. www.chicagoreader.com/chicago/the-man-behind-the-wall/Content?oid=894264.

At the time the Chicano Park murals were painted, the survival of Barrio Logan was in doubt. The city had constructed a freeway that split the neighborhood and also rezoned the neighborhood for industrial use, allowing several unsightly auto junkyards to set up shop. Residents were concerned that the new bridge would mean the demise of the neighborhood. As a concession, city leaders promised to preserve a sliver of parkland underneath the bridge for community use. When they later backed out of their promise and approved construction of a state police station and three-hundred-car parking lot on the site, residents were outraged. Together with college students from the area, they staged a protest in which they linked hands and refused to allow construction crews to dig up the park.

The idea of painting murals underneath the bridge came about as the second phase of the park resistance movement. A professional artist, Salvador Torres, who had been born and raised in Barrio Logan, negotiated with the bridge authorities

The murals at Chicano Park, under the San Diego-Coronado Bay Bridge in California, are inspired by the great Mexican murals of the 1920s.

to allow painting on its enormous concrete supports. Inspired by the great Mexican mural painters of the 1920s, Torres hoped the mural project would build civic pride and save the park from ruin. He recruited other young, idealistic Chicano artists from California and the southwest. As they laid out their paints and began to work, the scene was chaotic. Hundreds of enthusiastic non-artists in the community joined in, dipping their roller brushes in paint and haphazardly applying splashes of color to the towering concrete supports. Eventually themes emerged and the artists were permitted to direct the effort. They completed the first set of murals in 1974 in time for a joyous community dedication of Chicano Park, and added a second round in the early 1980s. The murals are bold, vibrantly colored, and openly political. They depict Aztec leaders, symbols, pyramids, religious motifs, Mexican revolutionary heroes, and figures from the Chicano resistance movement, including César Chávez, who fought for the rights of migrant farm workers.

Eco-Art: Raising Awareness of Environmental Issues

At roughly the same time that the Chicano artists were applying the last coats of paint to the murals beneath the Coronado Bridge, an artist across the country was creating a large-scale public art intervention (an artwork that attempts to change existing conditions) to call attention to world hunger and society's misguided use of environmental resources. For her work, *Wheatfield—A Confrontation*, artist Agnes Denes planted a wheat field within a few blocks of the Wall Street financial district, the heart of the country's banking industry and stock market. Denes was part of the growing Eco-Art movement, a term that covers a range of socially conscious artworks aimed at raising awareness about environmental issues, intervening to restore damaged lands, and promoting sustainability.

Wheatfield—A Confrontation was created in 1982 with support from the nonprofit Public Art Fund of New York. The

site was a trash-strewn landfill that Denes cleared with the help of two assistants and a corps of volunteers. Together they spread 224 truckloads of topsoil, planted two acres of wheat, and installed an irrigation system. In the summer, the wheat stalks stretched toward the sky, and in fall, they turned a golden yellow in stark contrast to the steel skyscrapers that surrounded the field. In late fall, Denes and her assistants harvested one thousand pounds of grain, which the artist felt represented the "tenacity of life"[34] because of its ability to grow and thrive even in the harshest of urban environments. Although the site was later converted into high-rise luxury buildings, Denes believed that her work left a lasting impression on city residents.

Artist and social activist Mel Chin also stages artistic interventions aimed at cleaning up damaged landscapes so they can support natural habitats. Chin's early art installations used a variety of media to convey strong messages about political or social issues. In 1990, he began work on a multi-year project called *Revival Field* that would become his most celebrated work of Eco-Art. *Revival Field* is located in the Pig's Eye Landfill in St. Paul, Minnesota, a site so loaded with toxic heavy metals that it posed a hazard to human health and was designated a "Superfund" or priority clean-up site by the U.S. government. Chin received support for his work from the Walker Art Center in Minnesota and the National Endowment for the Arts (although the agency first expressed concern that the project was more science than art). He collaborated with a U.S. government scientist to extract the heavy metals from a 60-square-foot (5.57 sq. m) patch of soil in the landfill. He began by surrounding the area of contaminated earth with a circular fence and dividing it into intersecting paths in an "x" pattern. In each section, he planted different varieties of plants that were known to absorb heavy metals through their leaves and roots. In the fall of 1991, the plants were harvested, dried, ground into ash, and tested. The plantings were then repeated until the soil was free of toxic materials. Art critics praised *Revival Field* as an innovative work that pushed the boundaries of public art.

Street Art: Trespassing on Public Spaces

If Eco-Art works like Chin's are about reclaiming degraded natural landscapes, another type of socially conscious public art aims to take back urban streets from private and commercial interests. Street Art is an unauthorized form of public art with roots in graffiti tagging, in which urban youth scrawl their names, or tags, in magic markers and aerosol spray paint to claim territory and bragging rights among their fellow taggers. The Street Art movement evolved as a hybrid of text-based graffiti tagging and visual art with a more openly social or political message. Artists with undercover aliases like Slink, Swoon, Banksy, Space Invader, and Blu use a range of visual styles and materials to create works of art that are aimed not at fellow artists or taggers, but at broad public audiences. They are not beholden to patrons, art critics, or government agencies, so they feel free to challenge authority. They place their works in derelict spaces, such as vacant lots or abandoned buildings, or hijack commercial billboards and old warehouses. The works last for a few hours, days, or weeks, depending on weather conditions and the whims of angry property owners or police, who often scrub the walls or rip them down. Yet because they are photographed and shared online, they become accessible to millions of people worldwide.

Shepard Fairey was one of the first street artists to capture worldwide attention in the 1990s with his graphic-art-inspired stickers depicting a stenciled image of a professional wrestler named Andre the Giant and the word "Obey." Stenciling is one of the most popular forms of Street Art, in which the artist uses appropriated images borrowed from commercial sources, alters and reproduces them, sometimes on a massive scale, and cuts them into stencils. The images can be quickly transferred to the wall using roller brushes or spray paint before the artist draws unwanted attention. Fairey plastered his "Obey" stickers on buildings around the world as part of a fake propaganda campaign. Although the images were meaningless, they became

A London, England, pedestrian walks by a 2006 spray-and-stencil artwork, *Sweeping It Under the Carpet,* attributed to graffiti artist Banksy.

BUT IS IT ART?

Few people would argue that a mass-produced poster found in a shopping mall or a statue in a Disney World theme park is public art, but what about a commemorative patchwork quilt hand sewn, painted, and stitched together; a circular garden of heavy-metal-eating plants in a toxic waste site; or stenciled drawings plastered on the side of abandoned buildings? Who determines what qualifies as public art and why?

Street artists reject the idea that art must be obscure or require an expert's interpretation to be important, or that its value should be determined by the price it fetches in the art market. They take their art directly to the streets to avoid these constraints.

Artist Mel Chin believes that public art should include projects that merge art with social awareness. In defending his work *Revival Field,* to the National Endowment for the Arts (NEA), he described it as "a conceptual artwork with an intent to sculpt a site's ecology."[1]

The NEA was persuaded by his description of a new kind of public art and agreed to sponsor the artwork. In the case of the *AIDS Memorial Quilt,* many of the people who contributed panels had never before in their lives felt confident about making art, and yet audiences across the country were deeply moved by the emotional power of the work. "Very few artists or art projects are able to reach so many people in such a way,"[2] writes art historian E.G. Crichton.

1. Quoted in Tom Finkelpearl. *Dialogues in Public Art.* Cambridge, MA: Massachusetts Institute of Technology Press, 2001: p. 385.

2. E.G. Crichton. "Is the NAMES Quilt Art?" In *Critical Issues in Public Art,* edited by Harriet F. Senie and Sally Webster. New York: HarperCollins, 1992, p. 293.

a worldwide sensation. All it took was hype, which was exactly Fairey's point.

London-based Banksy, whose real identity remains a mystery, is a street artist and prankster whose subversive art addresses social issues such as consumerism, violence, and government censorship—with a sharp sense of humor. He paints his signature rats and other stenciled figures, combined with satirical, anti-corporate, and anti-government slogans, on walls around the world. One of his most famous images shows a street protester, arm extended back as if to throw something—but instead of a rock or a grenade, he holds a bouquet of flowers. Banksy has also become famous for staging elaborate pranks that attract worldwide media attention. In 2005, he slipped past security guards at four of the most prestigious art museums in New York City, where he attached ornately framed copies of his street art in the exhibit halls.

Another street artist, New York-based Swoon, has a different social mission. She creates intricate, folk art–inspired paper cutouts of life-size human figures, which she pastes on old, crumbling walls in forgotten parts of the city. She spends months in her studio drawing her figures and creating wood block prints before transferring the images to newsprint, cutting them, and using wheat paste to post them up. Swoon wants her art to encourage people to engage in dialogue and take an active interest in the neglected public spaces around them.

Although there is a thrill for many street artists in trespassing on private property, climbing fences and rooftops, and hijacking commercial billboards, they make a strong distinction between their art and acts of vandalism. Their intention is to enhance their surroundings or raise awareness about social issues, not to deface private property. (The law does not make such a distinction and the artists are subject to fines and imprisonment for criminal trespass, vandalism, and destruction of property if they are caught.) From the point of view of Banksy, "The people who truly deface our neighborhoods are the companies that scrawl giant slogans across buildings and buses trying to make us feel inadequate unless we buy their stuff."[35] In recent years, many

SWOON: PAPER CUTOUTS IN FORGOTTEN CITY SPACES

Street artist Swoon started pasting her life-size, intricately-cut paper figures on the streets of New York City in 1999. Her portraits are based on people she knows or observes in the city. Sometimes they are rendered realistically—an elderly man sitting on a milk crate or a family feeding pigeons—and at other times as whimsical figures—a sea goddess or a man with a detailed cityscape in place of his body. Swoon spends hours in her studio drawing and creating woodblock prints of her work, hand-printing, and cutting them. She scouts her locations carefully, looking for forgotten spaces: warehouses, rundown buildings, and broken-looking walls. Her goal is to spark interest in rundown public spaces. Since her works are created on thin newsprint, it is not long before they tatter, peel, and decay. In recent years, her work has been featured in museums and galleries and she has begun to sell prints of her art. She uses the money to fund social and humanitarian work, which includes building boats from recycled materials and floating them down the Mississippi River and organizing a village in Haiti to build homes from recycled materials salvaged from the streets.

A street mural by Swoon is seen in the East End of London, England, in 2012.

street artists have become art-world celebrities. The irony of their success is not lost on them. They continue to mock the art world, even as their work fetches thousands of dollars.

When Audiences Become the Artists

Street artists often envision themselves as rebel crusaders, fighting to maintain public spaces for free expression and public dialogue. Another form of public art engages audiences even more directly by giving them an active role in the creative process from conception to finished product. Participatory public art often uses digital technology and social media as tools in its creation, but it also owes a debt to much earlier traditions, including the homespun collective craft-making that brought residents of small towns across America together to quilt, sew, or raise a barn together. Often, the process in which people come together to create participatory works of public art is as important as the finished product.

The *AIDS Memorial Quilt* is one of the largest and best-known community art projects in the world. The project began with a group of social activists in San Francisco who were searching for a way to commemorate friends and loved ones who had died of AIDS, the deadly disease that claimed millions of lives throughout the 1980s (effective treatments became available in the mid-1990s, but there is no cure yet). In the United States, the disease had a particularly devastating impact among homosexual men, and many people felt they would be stigmatized if they talked publicly about friends and loved ones whom they had lost. The quilt helped to remove that stigma.

The *AIDS Memorial Quilt* is a patchwork of 3-foot-by-6-foot (.91m × 1.8m) panels, each of which represents an individual who died of AIDS. Participants were given blank panels in memory of family members or loved ones. They sewed, painted, and adhered items to the fabric, including articles of clothing, teddy bears, photographs, stories and messages, along with the

names of those who died. The individual panels were then sewn together in a San Francisco workshop.

In 1987, the *AIDS Memorial Quilt* was displayed on the National Mall in Washington, D.C. for the first time. It covered a space larger than a football field and included more than nineteen hundred panels. Half a million people visited the Mall to see it. A year later, in 1988, the Quilt was displayed on the Mall again after a national tour that raised hundreds of thousands of dollars for AIDS service organizations. In 1996, when the entire quilt was displayed for the last time, its forty-four thousand panels covered the expanse of the National Mall. Its sheer size, and the size of the audiences who came to see it, were moving and powerful visual reminders of the millions of people from all walks of life who had been affected by the disease.

Artist and urban planner Candy Chang was also struggling to cope with the death of a close friend when she created a work of public art in 2011 called *Before I Die*. In the midst of her grief, Chang found that she was constantly thinking about the meaning of life and struggling to keep perspective. She wondered if

Parts of the *AIDS Memorial Quilt*, a community-driven art project in which each panel commemorates someone who has died from AIDS, is displayed at the National Mall in Washington, D.C., in 2012. The piece is now too large to be shown in any one place at one time.

other people experienced the same thoughts. Professionally, she had long been interested in creating new civic spaces in which people could connect and share ideas. With the help of several friends, Chang painted the side of an abandoned house in her New Orleans, Louisiana, neighborhood with black chalkboard paint and stenciled a grid with the sentence fragment "Before I Die I want to" followed by a series of blank spaces. Anyone passing by the wall could pick up a piece of chalk and share his or her personal dreams and aspirations. Within a day, every inch of space on the wall was covered with handwritten responses. Some were nonsensical: "Before I die I want to eat a salad with an alien." Others were ambitious: "sing for millions," "build a school," "go to Rome." Many more were profoundly moving: "hold her one more time," "see my daughter graduate."[36] The *Before I Die* wall was such a success that Chang created a toolkit with stencils and instructions so other communities could replicate the project.

A Public Space for Democracy

In the view of many artists and art historians, participatory, community-based projects like Chang's *Before I Die* wall represent the most important role that public art can play in modern American society. These interactive works of art promote democracy by capturing the spirit of "the commons": the central greens, public spaces, and squares that once existed in many American cities and towns, where people came together for planned events and spontaneous ones, to debate, rally, campaign, make speeches, celebrate, mourn, connect with each other, and share ideas. Even in an era of social media and online communication, the popular success of public artworks like *Before I Die* is a reminder that some of the most meaningful social interactions take place in public spaces in the physical world, rather than through a screen in the virtual one.

Notes

Introduction: Art for Everyone

1. Cher Krause Knight. *Public Art: Theory, Practice and Populism.* Malden, MA: Blackwell, 2008, p. ix.

Chapter 1: Evolving Ideas of Public Art

2. Knight. *Public Art*, p. 20.
3. Walt Whitman. "Ah, Not This Granite Dead and Cold." *The Philadelphia Press*, February 22, 1885. whitmanarchive.org/published/periodical/poems/per.00068.
4. Quoted in Marlene Park and Gerald E. Markowitz. *Democratic Vistas: Post Offices and Public Art in the New Deal.* Philadelphia: Temple University Press, 1984, p. 5.
5. Knight. *Public Art*, p. 5.
6. Quoted in Tom Finkelpearl. *Dialogues in Public Art.* Cambridge: Massachusetts Institute of Technology Press, 2000, p. 10.
7. Finkelpearl. *Dialogues in Public Art*, p. 23.
8. Erika Doss. "Public Art Controversy: Cultural Expression and Civic Debate." *Monograph*, October 2006, p. 2. artsusa.org/pdf/networks/pan/doss_controversy.pdf
9. Quoted in Jeff Becker. "Public Art: Essential Component of Creating Communities." *Monograph*, March 2004, p. 7. artsusa.org/pdf/networks/pan/becker_communities.pdf.

Chapter 2: Public Art in the City

10. Michael Kammen. *Visual Shock: A History of Art Controversies in American Culture.* New York: Alfred A. Knopf, 2006, p. 222.
11. Kammen. *Visual Shock*, p. 223.
12. Quoted in Regina Frank. "Sculpting Urban Airspace: Janet Echelman." *Sculpture*, September 2011, p. 1.
13. Quoted in Penny Balkin Bach. *Public Art in Philadelphia.* Philadelphia: Temple University Press, 1992, p. 161.
14. Quoted in Roberta Smith. "Scott Burton, Sculptor Whose Art Verged on Furniture, Is Dead at 50." *New York Times*, January 1, 1990, Obituaries.

Chapter 3: A New Way of Remembering the Past

15. Erika Doss. *Memorial Mania: Public Feeling in America.* Chicago: The University of Chicago Press, 2010, p. 27.
16. Quoted in Doss. *Memorial Mania*, p. 128.
17. Kirk Savage. *Monument Wars: Washington, D.C., the National Mall, and*

the Transformation of the Memorial Landscape. Berkeley: University of California Press, 2009, p. 261.

18. Quoted in Doss. Memorial Mania, p. 39.

19. Quoted in Adi Gordon and Amos Goldberg. "Holocaust Monuments and Counter-Monuments: Excerpt from Interview with Professor James E. Young." May 24, 1998, p. 6. www.yadvashem.org/odot_pdf /Microsoft%20Word%20-%203659 .pdf.

20. Quoted in Doss. Memorial Mania, p. 287.

21. Quoted in Doss. Memorial Mania, p. 289.

Chapter 4: Destination Public Art

22. Amy Dempsey. Destination Art. Berkeley: University of California Press, 2006, p. 8.

23. Quoted in the website of Roden Crater. www.rodencrater.com/about.

24. Knight. Public Art, p. 42.

25. Frank Rose. "Amarillo's Answer to Stonehenge." New York Times, January 11, 1987. www.nytimes .com/1987/01/11/travel/amarillo -s-answer-to-stonehenge.html?page wanted=print&rsc=pm.

26. Quoted in Arthur Lubow. "Andy Goldsworthy: Using Nature as His Canvas, the Artist Creates Works of Transcendent Beauty." Smithsonian, November 2005, p. 46.

27. Michael Kimmelman. "In a Saffron Ribbon, a Billowy Gift to the City." New York Times, February 13, 2005. www.nytimes.com/2005/02/13/arts /13kimmelman.html.

28. Doss. Memorial Mania, p. 185.

29. Kimmelman. "In a Saffron Ribbon, a Billowy Gift to the City." New York Times, February 13, 2005. www .nytimes.com/2005/02/13/arts /13kimmelman.html.

30. Quoted in Erika Niedowski. "Art Installation Highlights Fabric of R.I. City's Past." Boston Globe, January 9, 2012.

Chapter 5: Public Art with a Social Message

31. Anne Pasternak. "Just Do It." In Trespass: A History of Uncommissioned Urban Art. Edited by Ethel Seno. Koln, Germany: Taschen, 2010, p. 308.

32. Jenny Holzer. In "The Art History Archive—Biography and Art." www .arthistoryarchive.com/arthistory /contemporary/Jenny-Holzer.html.

33. Quoted in Phoebe Hoban. "Emancipation from War's Horrors." Wall Street Journal, November 12, 2012. http://online.wsj.com/article/SB1 00014241278873248941045781 05151602946238.html#articleTabs %3Darticle.

34. Don Krug. "Ecological Restoration— Agnes Denes, Wheatfield." Art and Ecology: Perspectives and Issues. http:// greenmuseum.org/c/aen/Issues /denes.php.

35. Garrett McAuliffe. "Banksy, Satirical Stenciling and a Graffiti Manifesto." Mission Local, May 2, 2010. http:// missionlocal.org/2010/05/who-the -heck-is-banksy.

36. "The Story, What Is Important to You?" Before I Die. http://beforeidie .cc/site/about.

Glossary

art-off-the-easel: A broad range of alternative art forms to emerge in the 1960s outside the realm of traditional museums or galleries, including Conceptual Art, Installation Art, Land Art, and Performance Art.

Conceptual Art: An art movement that originated in the 1960s in which the concept and processes involved in creating a work of art takes precedence over its aesthetic values.

Eco-Art: Socially conscious art aimed at raising awareness about environmental issues or in which artists intervene to repair damaged landscapes or promote ecological sustainability.

Environmental Art: An umbrella term that encompasses many different types of art focused on the environment, including socially-conscious Eco-Art, Land Art, and works created in natural landscapes or from natural materials.

figurative: Describes painting and sculpture that is representational and derived from real life.

Installation Art: Works in which audiences are immersed in a three-dimensional experience that stimulates the senses with objects, paintings, lights, sounds, and other media.

Land Art: Also called Earth Art or Earthworks, artworks that are often massive in scale and are built into natural landscapes such as deserts, mountains, and forests.

Minimalism: A movement in which artworks are pared down to their most essential, sparest forms.

Modernism: A twentieth-century art movement that discarded traditional techniques, such as perspective, composition, and color.

percent-for-art: A means of funding works of public art in which a percentage of construction costs for new buildings is set aside for the design or purchase of art.

Pop Art: An art movement that celebrates and satirizes mass culture by incorporating advertising images, comic books, and everyday household items.

site-specific: Works of art that are built for a specific location and take into account its uses, history, and environment.

Street Art: A countercultural movement with origins in graffiti tagging, in which artists place their visual art on the streets without permission from government agencies or private property owners.

Books

Michael Capek. *Murals: Cave, Cathedral, to Street*. Minneapolis, MN: Lerner, 1996. A historical overview of mural painting aimed at young adult readers. Describes community murals in the United States, then delves into earlier forms, including the Mexican murals of the 1920s, Renaissance frescoes, ancient Roman and Egyptian murals, and the prehistoric cave paintings of the Ice Age.

Amy Dempsey. *Destination Art*. Berkeley: University of California Press, 2006. A guide to two hundred of the world's landmark works of destination art with vibrant large-scale photos and descriptions of each work. Includes monumental works of Land Art in the American West such as *Spiral Jetty*, *Sun Tunnels*, and *Double Negative*.

Jan Greenberg and Sandra Jordan. *Christo and Jeanne-Claude: Through the Gates and Beyond*. New York: Roaring Brook, 2008. In dramatic photos and simple text, the authors explore the history and construction of Christo and Jeanne-Claude's enormous art installation *The Gates*, which transformed Central Park in New York City, and the fanfare surrounding the artwork.

Jan Greenberg and Sandra Jordan. *The Sculptor's Eye: Looking at Contemporary American Art*. New York: Delacorte, 1993. This book for young adult readers includes interviews with contemporary sculptors, photos of indoor and outdoor works by Claes Oldenburg, George Segal, Alexander Calder and many others, and descriptions of the creative processes and materials the artists use.

Sal Lopes. *The Wall: Images and Offerings from the "Vietnam Veterans Memorial."* New York: Collins, 1987. As a testament to the emotional power of Maya Lin's *Vietnam Veterans Memorial*, photojournalist Sal Lopes has assembled moving photos of veterans and other visitors at the Wall, along with text from the heartwrenching letters left in memory of loved ones and family members.

Milton Meltzer. *Violins and Shovels: The WPA Arts Projects*. New York: Delacorte, 1976. Historian Meltzer's first-person account of his experience and that of many struggling artists, musicians, actors, and writers who became part of the Depression-era New Deal arts programs, the most extensive ever undertaken by the federal government.

Websites

Judy Baca (www.judybaca.com). The official homepage of renowned Los Angeles-based muralist and social activist Judy Baca. Features a biography, photographs, and video clips of *The Great Wall of Los Angeles* and other community mural projects.

Ned Kahn (www.nedkahn.com). Homepage of environmental artist Ned Kahn, whose large-scale sculptural works combine science and art to showcase forces of nature such as wind, ocean waves, and tornados. Includes a biography and photographs of Kahn's dynamic artworks.

Claes Oldenburg and Coosje van Bruggen (www.oldenburgvanbrug gen.com). Homepage for Claes Oldenburg, the world's most celebrated Pop Art sculptor, and his late partner and collaborator, Coosje van Bruggen. Features photos of their whimsical Pop Art sculptures, including *Clothespin*, *Batcolumn*, *Spoonbridge and Cherry*, and many others.

PBS Art21 (www.pbs.org/art21). This website is associated with the award-winning public television series *Art in the Twenty-First Century* and features short video documentaries that introduce contemporary artists and their works, including Jenny Holzer, Krzysztof Wodiczko, Maya Lin, James Turrell, and Richard Serra. (A list of artists appears on the Video page of the site.)

Roden Crater (www.rodencrater.com). The homepage for James Turrell's monumental work of Land Art and naked-eye observatory carved into an extinct volcanic crater in the Painted Desert of Arizona. Includes photos of the viewing chambers inside the crater and a video interview with the visionary artist.

Swoon, Street Art Video (www.time out.com/london/art/exclusive -swoon-street-art-video). A short-format video that follows street artist Swoon as she talks through the creative process involved in one of her elaborate paper cut figures. In time-lapse photography, she is shown pasting the figure beneath a railway bridge in London.

Index

Picture Credits

About the Author

Meryl Loonin is a young adult book author who has written four previous titles for Lucent. She lives with her husband, Neil, and two teenage children, Hana and Jonah, in her hometown of Lexington, Massachusetts. For *Public Art*, Loonin discovered many intriguing works of art, including the Chicano Murals in San Diego, where she grew up. She hopes readers will be inspired to look for public art in their own cities and towns.